MW01231710

# STOP
## the VIOLENCE...
### *Seven Stages to Sanctify*

## Claim the Promises of Christ

Workbook for "Journey of the Soul...Cracked Pots and Broken Vessels...
Live the Victorious Life Christ Died to Give You." Grow in maturity by
facing problems and challenges of life in a fallen world

## DR. PHYLLIS DAVIS *and*
## REV. CARROL DAVIS

PRESS

The Scripture versions cited in this book are identified as follows:

KJV – King James Version

NKJV – New King James Version

NIV – New International Version

AMP – Amplified Bible

RSV – Revised Standard Version

# "STOP THE VIOLENCE…

# SEVEN STAGES TO

# SANCTIFY

*Claim the promises of Christ"*

DR. PHYLLIS DAVIS *and*
REV. CARROL DAVIS

# *STOP THE VIOLENCE...SEVEN STAGES TO SANCTIFY...*
## *Claim the Promises of Christ©*

# TABLE OF CONTENTS

# FORWARD

*"He told them this parable: "No one tears a patch from a new garment and sews it on an old one. If he does, he will have torn the new garment, and the patch from the new will not match the old. And no one pours new wine into old wineskins. If he does, the new wine will burst the skins, the wine will run out and the wineskins will be ruined. No, new wine must be poured into new wineskins. And no one after drinking old wine wants the new, for he says, 'The old is better.'"* Luke 5:36-39 NIV

In the Scriptures the Pharisees are compared to old wine skins in that they could not receive the teachings of Jesus because they were so steeped in the laws and traditions of their day. They feared the teachings of Jesus, were jealous of His knowledge, miracles and signs. They feared they would lose control of the people if the people did not look to the priest and leaders for their spiritual guidance. Today is no different. Many leaders of the church preach a personal walk with the Savior and can not model it. Their testimonies speak of their salvation experience, not a daily walk with the Savior.

The Pharisees were like many of our modern day church leaders: Like old wine skins, they can not receive new wine with out bursting. Many modern day churches, like the Pharisees can not receive new approaches to the teaching of the gospel. Steeped in the traditions, cultural norms, pathology of men, they deny the power of the risen, living Jesus. They speak of a personal relationship with Christ and yet have not even one testimony to testify to their walk with Jesus today. In any relationship, including one with the Savior, time is required. Jesus wants us to share our needs, our challenges, and our accomplishments, relying on Him for the very breath we take, giving Him the credit and the glory. Nothing happens to us, good or bad, that is not sifted through the loving hands of Jesus.

Our pride, addictions, accomplishments, position, power, abuse and lack of knowledge turn us away from the living Jesus to glorify our own names, having a form of Godliness but denying the power thereof. We piously claim we are "fine" when under the privacy of our own roofs we struggle with many issues. "Christians are not supposed to have problems." We buy into the lies of Satan and refuse to acknowledge our humanness.

Jesus sweated blood, prayed throughout the night, went to the disciples to request prayer, and asked our Heavenly Father to take the cup from Him if at all possible, and He was the perfect God/man. Yet we, with our prideful attitudes, claim we are not broken. We deceive ourselves and prevent the ability to live the victorious life Christ died to give us.

In the great commission, we are admonished by Christ Himself to teach all that He taught us. Discipleship is part of the commission requirements, yet many churches and their leaders point to the numbers to justify their effectiveness: How many were baptized? How many joined this Sunday? How much growth have we accomplished this year? How many buildings did we build?

We are focused on different numbers: How many people fall away from the faith because they are not taught how to rightly apply the word of God to their present need(s)? How many affairs go on in the church on a weekly basis? How many separations are your church members dealing with? How much divorce is in the middle of your congregation? How many women were beaten this week without as much as a phone call from a church member? How many children are beaten half to death in the name of Christ, without our notice and/or intervention? How much addiction to prescription medication are your members experiencing because of their lack of knowledge? How much money was embezzled from your church funds due to the addiction of a trusted member? What has the Church done to assist the rehabilitation for that member's family? How many people sit on the front row of your church, and attend regularly, yet have no personal relationship with Christ? They believe they are saved. They grew up in the church. They attend regularly and even teach Sunday school; yet they do not have nor understand a personal walk with the Savior. They are not taught how to rightly apply the word of God to their lives and the challenges of living in a fallen world.

We believe the church is being called to a new era, an era in which the power of the risen Christ is relied on to heal the sick, and part the "Red Sea" of Christian problems, reflective of His power to overcome. We believe the church is being called to an honest assessment of individual lives, leaders, talents, assets and abilities as well as character defects in order to heal and truly live the abundant lives Christ died to give us. We are being called to live out the Scriptures, building up the saints, and the church united in the faith, all faiths, not Baptist, Methodist, Lutheran, Unitarian; but Christians, and ambassadors of Christ. We believe this is the new "Revival."

This workbook is designed to accompany the book *"Journey of the Soul...Cracked Pots and Broken Vessels...Live the Victorious Life Christ Died to Give You"* and to take you, the reader, on a personal journey to apply the words of the Master to specific areas of challenge in your life. The techniques used in the workbook are tested principles of sound psychological living from the Mighty Counselor, Great Physician and His word to us through His love letter, the Scriptures.

Different from most "talk therapies" the techniques used are experiential in nature, addressing the right brain and the unconscious mind, using the model *"SEVEN STAGES TO SANCTIFY"* Copyright 1993, 1995, revised 2013, 2014© *"Journey of the Soul...Cracked Pots and Broken Vessels...Live the Victorious Life Christ Died to Give You"* is about the *sanctification* process, the journey of the soul from a life of dis-ease and dysfunction to the life you were meant to live. The workbook will be most helpful if you read the book first, followed by the exercises in the workbook. We hope *"Journey of the Soul....Cracked Pots and Broken Vessels..."* and *"STOP THE VIOLENCE ...SEVEN STAGES TO SANCTIFY... Claim the Promises of Christ"* serve as discipleship tools to help individuals on their journey of discovery and to guide the process. Christians and teachers then work together toward the common goal of healing, growing more like Christ.

*"STOP THE VIOLENCE...SEVEN STAGES TO SANCTIFY...Claim the Promises of Christ"* and *"Journey of the Soul...Cracked Pots and Broken Vessels...Live the Victorious Life Christ Died to Give You,"* are written to the church and fellow Christians that want to mature in Christ receiving all of the

blessings He died to give. If you have not accepted Christ as your Savior, you are not filled with the Holy Spirit, and you do not have the power of the living Jesus coursing through your veins. Receiving Christ is easy, it is free and it is available to *"whosoever will,"* so if you have not accepted Jesus as your Lord and Savior, we need to settle that issue first. If you are not sure, then tell Jesus and let Him know that you want to be certain. We don't want to embarrass anybody. We will not call attention to you. We will ask everyone to follow along as we read the prayer for salvation. If you truly want to be saved, and have not done so, God judges the motives of a heart and he will hear your cry for salvation, and honor your prayer.

> *"If you confess with your mouth Jesus as Lord, and believe in your heart that God raised Him from the dead, you will be saved." Romans 10:9 "For by grace you have been saved through faith; and that not of yourselves, it is the gift of God, not as a result of works, so that no one may boast." Ephesians 2:8, 9 KJV*

**Prayer for Salvation, Forgiveness, Guidance, Filling of the Holy Spirit**

*Heavenly Father,*

*I come before your throne of grace thanking you for sending your Son Jesus in the flesh, the perfect God/ Man to die on the cross for my sins. I confess my sin(s) and my sinful nature to you and ask that you forgive me and wash me white as snow with the blood of the lamb, slain for me. Father, you say that salvation is my free gift, available to anyone that believes that Jesus is your son, He died on the cross for my sins, and the third day He arose from the dead. I agree that I have sinned and need a Savior. I accept my free gift of salvation; I turn from my sin and self to Jesus. I ask Jesus to be my Lord and Savior. Father, some are not sure if they have truly been saved. They have said the prayer before, yet they still have doubts. Father I ask that you accept their plea of Salvation and that you make the Holy Spirit's presence in their lives so strong that they can never doubt again, for the Holy Spirit is our guarantee of eternal life to come, the power to convict of sin, and the power to heal and overcome the sin of this world. Thank you Father for all you have done and all you are going to do. I ask you to go with me on this journey to receive the gift of healing and the abundance your son died to give me. It is in His precious name I pray, Amen.*

We hope that the process will help religious leaders make the Scripture come alive as God's love letter to you. We hope that the Bible becomes the beloved book it was meant to be, an instruction Book to navigate life's storms. It is our hope you find freedom in the process as the God of truth transforms your life and you fall more in love with your "ABBA Father."

# AUTHORS' NOTES

All of the characters' names have been changed to protect their identities and confidentiality. Names of towns, people, places, and some things have been changed to further protect the individuals involved. The stories and case histories are all true and reflect true treatment goals, presenting problems and the procedures followed.

Actual treatment records have been used with permission: to educate, illustrate and tell the story, in order to help others on their individual journeys. The names of the individuals have been changed at the authors' discretion, even though permission has been granted to reveal the true identity of the participants.

Personal stories are told from the authors' point of view and perspective and might or might not be the viewpoints of other individuals. Authors' personal experiences might or might not be reflective of the experiences of others.

All materials are copyrighted and cannot be reproduced in any form without express written permission from the authors'.

Editorial comments and suggestions are reflected in the use of the subject, "you" and the pronoun "you" in the plural form for consistency instead of the subject and pronouns: "me," "our," "us," and "we."

Authors' acknowledge that this book, its contents, instructions, and promises were given to us first to apply to our own lives. *"For all have sinned and come short of the glory of God." Romans 3:23 KJV "If we confess our sins, he is faithful and just to forgive us our sins, and to cleanse us from all unrighteousness."*

*1 John 1: 9 KJV.* We have applied these principles, to the best of our abilities and continue to pray for our Heavenly Father to sanctify all areas of our lives, transforming us into the creatures we were designed to become. Unless otherwise noted, all quotations are from the KJV translation. Thanks for allowing us to share our journeys with you.

Copyrighted materials reproduced in this material with permission of the parties holding the copyrights.

# ACKNOWLEDGEMENTS

Thanks to our parents for giving us life, for raising us and doing the very best they knew how, given the knowledge, information, and training they received. For the good traits you passed on to us, we are eternally grateful. For the traits that we consider "negative," we forgive you and release you in the name of Christ.

To our children, Nancy, Susan, Colleen and Sean, that were raised by two "cracked pots" and "broken vessels" we pray that God will instill the good and lead you to forgive the bad. We love you, bless you and pray you will become the creatures God created you to be, in spite of our misguided human attempts at parenting. May the power of God lift you up where you believe you were betrayed? May you find in your hearts the power of God to forgive us where we have failed? We pray you grow in His image, not ours.

To friends, associates, ex-wives and husbands, those we have hurt on the journey, we humbly ask your forgiveness and pray that God will heal any wounds we have caused and lead you to become all He created you to be.

We pray that our God will continue to sanctify you in His power and glory moving you on to become the people that He intended. We pray that our lives will be living amends to those we have harmed. We hope and pray that at the end our lives you will have seen more of Him in us and less of us. We pray we will have given Him the honor and glory and that when we approach His throne, we will hear, *"Well done good and faithful servant(s)." Matthew 25:21*

Thanks to our Pastors Dr. Rob Jackson and Dr. Paul Fleming for the opportunities to serve our Lord and Savior in church and the community. Dr. Al and Evelyn Snyder, and other fellow travelers for your loving support, kind words of encouragement, spiritual leadership, ideas, contributions, and sharing your testimonies, thank you.

Acknowledgements to our pastors: Perry Duggar, David Hardy and Ike Patterson for their encouragement and dedication to the *sanctification* process through discipleship training, mentoring, counseling and recovery programs.

Thank you to our friends for their support in missions, encouragement, and their kind words. We give a special thank you to Pastor Johnny Baker and Jan for their belief in our work, friendship, and the start on our journey together.

Special thanks to our sponsors and mentors, who have followed us, advised us, confronted us, exhorted, and encouraged us: Chaplain John Smith, Chaplain Al Sherbert, Chaplain Jim Gunn, Rev. James Ellis Griffeth, Nancy, Charlie Stobaugh, Mark, Sarah, Deb Evans, Pastor Ike Patterson, Sharon Spivey, Rev. Larry Spivey, and Pastor Johnny and Jan Baker.

Thanks to our editors, Sarah Lynch, Dr. Al and Evelyn Snyder, and to our friends at Xulon Press whose help, prayers, and kind words made this workbook possible.

With love, admiration, and awe we bow before the throne of our Lord Jesus. This book is all about Him and the marvelous work He does in our lives when we look to Him and allow Him to give us the abundant life. We pray that we will continue to be transformed by the power of His presence in our lives. We ask that His will be worked out in our hearts and minds as He transforms us into the people He intended in His creation, fulfilling the purposes of His design.

We acknowledge our grandchildren: Furman, Ciarra, Brianna, and Alexa. We thank God for the gift of your lives. We pray that you will seek the Lord and His guidance early in your lives and that you live under His protection, becoming the people that He created you to be. We pray that we will live to see you carry out His legacy of service and be blessed by the Lord Jesus Christ.

# INTRODUCTION:

## "Salvation" and "Sanctification."
### *Do You Know The Difference?*

*"Work out your salvation with fear and trembling." Philippians 2:12 KJV*

" *S*alvation" and *"Sanctification:"* Salvation is a one time event where you invite Christ to be the Lord of your life. Sanctification is an ongoing process where you invite the Holy Spirit to mold and shape each area of your life, to transform you from glory to glory, to become more like your Savior. Each area of your life that the Holy Spirit has sanctified becomes one more testimony to God's glory and to your good.

Trauma, abandonment, neglect, physical, sexual, emotional, intellectual and spiritual abuse are the characteristics underlying dysfunction of the families in America; diametrically opposed to the characteristics of Christ, the fruit of the spirit: love, joy, peace, patience, kindness, gentleness, goodness, faith, and self control. Your children live in homes infused with the influence of the sin pattern, the *"dark side."*

Most families consider their family "fairly normal," yet statistics point to the fact that ninety percent of the families in America are dysfunctional. Dysfunction is handed down from one generation to the next: *the sins of the father will be passed on to the second, third and fourth generations. Exodus 20:5, 34: 6-7. Deuteronomy 5:9, KJV. "For all have sinned, and come short of the glory of God." Romans 3:23 KJV* Before you let yourself off the hook, know that the other ten percent are in the *sanctification* process.

The question is not, "is my family dysfunctional?" Rather, "Specifically how is my family dysfunctional and how has that dysfunction affected my journey?" The effect of covenant broken with God is handed down, the children will suffer; yet each one is responsible for their own actions and reactions. Examples of this are in addictions: The alcoholic father's sins, break covenant with God by his actions, the disease is handed down. Each child can choose to drink or not, they are responsible for their own righteousness.

Children grow up with the mental picture of Jesus Christ having the face and characteristics of their fathers. Churches and religious leaders encourage you to trust, follow, and turn your life over to this image pointing to the Scripture as the way to live your life successfully. What if your father was abusive? Did he exhibit the loving, nurturing character traits of Christ? If not, what effect did that influence have on your life and relationship with Christ? What about the influence of your mother. Did she set a good example? Was Jesus Christ first in her life? Remember that this is the foundation on which your life was built. Was it built on "the rock" or sinking sand? This is where your journey begins.

*"...He leads me on paths of righteousness, He restores my soul..." 23rd Psalms*

## PRAYER

*Heavenly Father, Holy Spirit, I invite you into my process to lead me on the paths of righteousness. I pray that you will restore my soul to be in perfect alignment with your will and your ways. Father, you know everything that has ever happened to me and you know my areas of brokenness. Shine your light of knowledge and wisdom on these areas of brokenness; remove the scales from my eyes so that I can be keenly aware of the areas you wish to sanctify in my life. I will give you the praise and glory. In Jesus name I pray. Amen*

If your life is not filled with "the joy of thy salvation," you have areas of your life that are in bondage. The promises of God are not reflected in your life and you may be experiencing that bondage in several of the following areas. Circle all that apply to you and your family.

**IDOLATRY**: Any time people, places or things take the place in your life that is designed for God you are practicing idolatry:

| | | | | | | |
|---|---|---|---|---|---|---|
| Football | Soccer | Baseball | Basketball | Tennis | Golf | Boating |
| Shopping | Dancing | Exercising | Television | Computers | Fishing | Hunting |
| Motocross | Hang-gliding | Parasail | Money | Power | Position | |

The Holy Spirit might have convicted you of an area we have not mentioned, if so write it in here:

_____

**HURTS/HABITS/HANG-UPS**: Any time a behavior hurts you or others, becomes destructive to your relationship with God or others you might be experiencing one or more of the following. Circle all of the following areas that apply to you and your family.

Procrastination        Constantly Late        Constantly Early        Gossip        Tale Bearing

Broken Promises        Hypocritical Actions/Behaviors        Cursing/ Foul Mouth        Cheating

Alienation        Negative Self Image        Hyper-Alertness        Flashbacks / Nightmares

Exaggerating Truth/ Lying        Nail Biting        Hair Pulling        Cutting        Poor Hygiene

Fear of Rejection        Fear of Anger        Isolation        Fear of Being Alone        Problems Sleeping

Fear of Death        Quarreling/Fighting        Jealousy/Envy        Sarcasm        Complaining

Fear of Failure        Fear of the Unknown        Fear of Confrontation        Other Fears

The Holy Spirit might have convicted you of an area we have not mentioned, if so write it in here:

_____

**PROBLEMS/LIFE EXPERIENCES**: Many times, the problems of life over which you have no control can create stress and throw you into distress. Circle the problem(s) that might be creating stress in your life or the life of a family member.

Divorce / Separation          Chronic Illness          Loss of a Loved One          Death

Relationship Issues          Marital Problems          Parenting Problems          Care-Giver Problems

Loss of a Friend /Loss of a Pet          Loss of a Job          Financial Burdens          Legal Problems

Loss of Interest in Work or Activities          Problems with Intimate Relationships

Difficulty with Authority Figures          Emotional Distance from Wife/Children

Problems at Work          Pride          False Humility          Volunteering          Laziness          Busyness/Driven

Self Centered          Perfectionist          Anger Issues          Abortion          Rebellion

The Holy Spirit might have convicted you of an area we have not mentioned, if so write it in here:

_____

**SIN/DISOBEDIENCE TO GOD'S LAWS & COMMANDS:** Any time you break God's laws, commandments and are disobedient, you are in need of forgiveness, reconciliation, and turning your life around. Your history may include several of the following areas. Circle all of the areas that apply to you and your family members.

Womanizing    Adultery    Fornication    Rape    Incest    Sodomy    Robbery    Greed    Murder

Slander/Gossip         Drunkenness         Gluttony         Strife         Parental Disobedience

Tale Bearing        False Witness         Murder        Witchcraft        Sorcery        Envy Homosexual

Un-forgiveness         Table Lifting         Believing Lies         Roots of Bitterness         Liars

Foul Mouth Reviler        Extortion        Cheat        Bestiality        Swindler        Sex with the dead

Lasciviousness         Variance         Wrath         Envy         Impure/ Immoral Thoughts/Behavior

Unclean        Seditions        Hate        Emulations         Heresies         Magic Arts  Horoscopes

Palm Reading        Channeling        Astral Projection         Hoarding         Seance        Spells/Curses

Fortune Telling         Astrology         Some Video Games         Crystals or Pyramids

Ouija Board        Automatic Writing        Tarot Cards        Spirit Guides        Blood Pact        Magic 8 Ball

Mind Control         Wicca         Satanism         Black/White Magic         Superstitions

Blood Pacts         Occult Games/Practices         Rebellion against God / His Law(s)

Idolatry: Worship of the Gods of Money, Power, Position, Material Things, People, Status

The pride of life: I am the best teacher, preacher, accountant, salesman, student, mechanic, etc. I am irreplaceable. I am the most handsome, prettiest, most skilled, etc.

The Holy Spirit might have convicted you of an area we have not mentioned, if so write it in here:

_____

**ADDICTIONS**: It is not when you use, what you use, or how much you use. It is what using does to you and your life that causes the use to be out of control. It can affect one area or all areas of your life: work, home, spiritual, relationships, and/ or your health. Addictions usually come in threes. Once you have identified one, you might look for the other two. Use does not have to be immoral or illegal to be addiction. Addiction affects the entire family and each member needs to address the affects on their individual life. If you are not the addict, but you live with or love an addict, circle the "drug of choice" affecting your life. You are called the co-addict. If your parents are addicts, you are an adult/child. Circle the areas of addiction(s) affecting you or your family from the following list:

Alcohol          Drugs          Prescription Meds          Street Drugs          Gambling          Sex

Destructive Relationships          Religion          Shopping          Pornography          Love Addiction

Co-dependency          Electronic Gadgets          Work a holism          Sugar Carbohydrates          Caffeine

Exercise          Food          Jewelry          Shoes          Clothes          Womanizing          Sports

Adrenalin Rush          People          Power/Control          Places

The Holy Spirit might have convicted you of an area we have not mentioned, if so write it in here:

_____

**\*PHYSICAL DISEASES**: Physical problems must first be treated by a medical doctor. Many times addressing the underlying issues resolves physical manifestations of those issues. We have personally witnessed the phenomena in the following areas:

Migraine Headaches          Muscle Disorders          Chronic Pain          Vision Problems          Backaches

Cancer          Heart Disease          Broken Bones          Fibromyalgia          Blindness

Restless Leg Syndrome          Irritable Bowel Syndrome          Stomach Problems          Crones          Arthritis

High/Low Blood Pressure          Panic Attacks          Somatic Pain          Memory Impairment          Obesity

The Holy Spirit might have convicted you of an area we have not mentioned, if so write it in here:

_____

**PSYCHIATRIC DISORDERS** can manifest in the above forms of physical symptoms as well as the psychiatric diagnosis. The following is a partial list from the diagnostic manual of psychiatric disorders. The model has been successfully applied to most all of the psychiatric disorders listed with the exception of sociopathic disorders. While helpful, the success with this patient population is still unknown. These disorders are:

Depression        Anxiety        Anorexia        Bulimia        Thin/Fat Disorder        Phobias

Panic Attacks        Obsessive/Compulsive Disorders        Dissociative Disorder        Seizures

Gender Identity Disorder        Dissociative Identity Disorder        Eating Disorder        Manic-Depressive Disorder

Bi Polar Disorder        Conduct Disorder        Borderline Personality Disorder        MPD

Sleep Disorders        Thought Disorders        Addictions        Schizoaffective Disorde

Paranoia        Social Phobias and Fears        Pyromania        Multiple Sclerosis        Schizophrenia

Cynicism        Anger Issues        Psychic/Emotional Numbing        Survivor Guilt

Conduct Disorder        Suicidal Thoughts        Post Traumatic Stress Disorders

The Holy Spirit might have convicted you of an area we have not mentioned, if so write it in here:

_____

In the above examples your life is out of control if focused on any of the above and you hear complaints from family, friends and associates about time, attention, focus and money associated with any of the above. God is not at the center. Your priorities are out of order. Your life is out of balance. You neglect areas of your life that need and deserve your attention.

The Lord, Jesus told the Apostle Paul:

*"I am sending you to them to open their eyes and turn them from darkness to light and from the power of Satan to God, so that they may receive forgiveness of sins and a place among those who are sanctified by faith in me." Acts 26:17b, 18 NIV*

The following model is designed to allow maturity in Christ for Christians as you apply the seven stages to the areas of your life that you want Christ to transform. Submitting to the process invites Christ into areas of your life that look more like the world than Christ. Those seeking Christian maturity can look at their lives, look at the areas where Christ is at work and join Him there.

It is this process of transformation, the *sanctification* process that allows Christ to bless you with the abundant life of His promises. Like salvation, the gift of *sanctification* is free. Christ already paid the price when he shed his blood and died on the cross for your sins. You must be willing to submit to the process. Christ is a gentleman and He does not barge into any area of your life where He is not invited. Invite Him into your process and watch as he transforms your life and turns your scars to stars, your morning to dancing.

**Prayer**

*Heavenly Father, Holy Spirit I thank you for this time together to support each other in growing and maturing in you. I thank you for your Son, Jesus that died on the cross, shed his blood, and rose again to save me from my sins. I thank you Father, that I am numbered among those that will inherit the throne with Jesus.*

*Father, I come before your throne of grace asking to grow to be more like you, using your Son Jesus as my role model. I know that there are areas of my life that look more like the world than Jesus. I know that it is only through the power of the living Jesus that I can be sanctified and healed.*

*Father, I ask that you give me your wisdom and discernment to identify any areas of my life that are broken and need sanctifying. Just as your servant David prayed for you to search his heart to see if there was anything that was not pleasing to you, I ask you to search my heart. Show me areas of brokenness that you wish to sanctify and heal.*

*I ask you to take the scales off my eyes so that I can see clearly. Unstop my ears so that I can hear the gentle leading of the Holy Spirit as I submit my areas of brokenness to you. I pray that by the grace of Jesus, and the stripes He bore on His back, I will be healed.*

*Thank you Father for all you have done in my life and all you are going to do. I will give you the praise and glory.*

*Amen*

**Exercise**

*In the back of your workbook, you will find an intake sheet. This information is confidential, to be used to facilitate your work in group. No one will see this information except for the leaders of the workshop trained to facilitate the process of *SANCTIFICATION*. Each member must sign the agreement to the confidentiality form to participate. If you have questions or concerns, raise your hand in the small group and a facilitator will come to address your concerns.

Break up into groups of four. Take turns identifying the areas where you think Christ might want to grow and *sanctify* you. Share with the group your findings from each category of the circled list from above. Start with one category header and work around the group. Then go to the next category and so on until each group member has shared their findings from each category. The items circled in the category might reflect the actions and behavior of a family member or a loved one that has affected you. Make a note of that on your work sheet and share with your group.

The categories listed above are: psychiatric disease, physical disease, addictions, sin, disobedience to God's laws and commands, life experiences/problems, hurts, habits and hang-ups, idolatry. The categories listed below are the sub-categories. These are the items we are sharing in small group. If you wish to skip this exercise, you may do so. If you feel more comfortable sharing from the category heading only, you might share the heading of the category that troubles you. Tell the group you choose to share at a later time, when you feel more comfortable, and listen to the others as they share.

Save your lists and your findings, we will be discussing them later. If you get stuck, or have trouble getting started, raise your hand and one of the leaders will come to your group to help you get started. If there is an issue in your family that is not on the list, you can add the item you wish to address. The lists are to help you get started and are not exhaustive. Remember that what you share in this class and the group work that you do is confidential. We are here to support each other in maturing in Christ. Gossip and tale bearing are not acceptable. Failure to comply with these instructions is grounds for removal from the group. We appreciate your co-operation.

## OVERVIEW

God uses *"cracked pots and broken vessels"* to tell His story.*"They overcame him by the power of the blood of the lamb and the word of their testimony and they loved not their lives unto death." Revelation 12:11 KJV*

*"Salvation"* is an event, an experience, a time in your life when you invite Jesus Christ into your heart to save you from your sin and self and give you eternal life. *Sanctification* is a process over time. It is the process whereby you allow the Lord of your life to transform you, to shape and mold you into the creature He created you to become. The process continues throughout the life of the Christian, daily, as you grow and mature in Christ to become more like Him in every area of your life.

God doesn't waste anything or anyone. If you let Him, He can take the scars and pain of your life and turn you into the vessel of His glory you were created to become. Nothing surprises God. He knows that you sin and fall short of His glory and He has a plan to redeem you, save you and let His light shine through you. His power is made perfect in your weaknesses. When you are the weakest, He is the strongest. God uses the pain and confessed sin in your life to build your character, equip you for His purpose and mission, to guide you, to correct you, to heal you and to make you more like Him.

Many Christians and most Churches focus on the evangelism of the un-churched looking to the number of those that make a decision for Christ and those that are baptized, as if these numbers reflect obedience to the "Great Commission."

In the Scripture Christ says, *"If you love me, you will obey me,"* and the *"Great Commission"* speaks of discipleship. Yet many Christians walk in bondage for failure to know, and follow the word of God. Practical application of the word of God is very seldom taught and adhered to. Compartmentalized Christianity is more the norm than an exception. Religious addiction of going through the motions on Sunday as a part of the Christian life is most common, even among devout believers. You check it off of your weekly "to do list," as done. You are complacent in your walk with Christ. Christ says, *"So then because thou art lukewarm, and neither cold nor hot, I will spue thee out of my mouth." Revelation 3:16*

The Bible is God's love letter to you, an instruction book to guide you through all of life's difficulties. Who better to lead, guide and direct you through uncertain times than the one who knows all, is everywhere, and knows of the best plans for your life? Yet as Scripture says, *"My people are destroyed for lack of knowledge." Hosea 4:6 KJV*

It is only when Christ becomes the Lord of your life, you seek to know Him more, following all of His commandments, that you can start to live the victorious life in a fallen world. When you truly mean, *"Thy will be done in earth as it is in Heaven,"* you get out of the drivers seat and look to the *"...author and finisher of our faith." (Matthew 6:10 KJV, Hebrews 12:2 a KJV)*

> *"SANCTIFICATION" is that relationship with God into which men enter by faith in Christ. 1 Corinthians 6:11 and Acts 26:18. (Vines) and* Jesus talks to Saul *"To open their eyes, and to turn them from darkness to light, and from the power of Satan unto God, that they may receive forgiveness of sins and inheritance among them which are 'SANCTIFIED BY FAITH' that is in me." Acts 26:18 KJV*

Sanctification is also used in the New Testament to speak of the separation of the believer from evil things and ways. This sanctification is God's will for the believer:

> *"For this is the will of God, even your sanctification that ye should abstain from fornication: That every one of you should know how to posses his vessel in sanctification and honor." 1 Thessalonians 4:3, 4 KJV*

Paul writes, in his letter to the Christians at Philippi:

> *"Therefore my dear ones as you have always obeyed (my suggestions) so now not only (with enthusiasm you would show) in my presence but much more because I am absent, work out (that is cultivate, carry out to the goal and fully complete your own salvation with*

*reverence and awe) self distrust, with serious caution, tenderness of conscience, watchfulness against temptation, timidly shrinking from whatever might offend God and discredit the name of Christ." Philippians 2:12 AMP*

Paul later advises the saints of Corinth:

*"For though we walk, that is live in the flesh , we are not carrying on our warfare according to the flesh and using mere human weapons. For the weapons of our warfare are not physical weapons of flesh and blood, but they are mighty before God, for the overthrow and destruction of strongholds, in as much as we refute arguments, and theories, and reasoning, and every proud and lofty thing that sets itself up against the true knowledge of God and we lead every thought and purpose away captive into the obedience of Christ." 2 Corinthians 10:3-6 AMP*

You inherited the "intergenerational sin" when you were born on the planet. You were born into a "sinful" world. The question is not, "do you have issues?" The question is, "specifically what are your issues and how have they affected your lack of the abundant life Christ died to give you?" ***"Journey of the Soul... Cracked Pots and Broken Vessels"*** combines sound principles of psychology, sociology, and recovery with the teachings of the Master to apply the truth of God's word to life's problems and challenges in the *"sanctification process."* The journey starts after your commitment to Christ, the "salvation" experience. The seven stage model, ***"SEVEN STAGES TO SANCTIFY,"*** and the workbook, ***"STOP THE VIOLENCE...SEVEN STAGES TO SANCTIFY...Claim the Promises of Christ,"*** allow you to submit problem areas of your life to the process in order to receive the healing and transformation Christ died to give you. They are discipleship tools that help you receive the abundant life Christ meant for you to have.

# Seven Stages of the Journey and the Biblical Comparisons:

# SANCTIFY©

*"Work out your salvation with fear and trembling." Philippians 2:12 KJV*

*S*alvation and *Sanctification: Salvation* is a one time event where you invite Christ to be the Lord of your life. *Sanctification* is an ongoing process where you invite the Holy Spirit to mold and shape each area of your life, to transform you from glory to glory, to become more like your Savior. Each area of your life that the Holy Spirit has sanctified becomes one more testimony to God's glory and to your good.

*S Strongholds / Besetting Sins / Problem State*

*I admit that there are strongholds, besetting sins or problems that I would like healed. There are areas of my life that do not look like Christ.*

*IDENTIFYING THE PROBLEM(S)*

Physical Disease, Psychiatric Disease, Addictions, Strongholds, Besetting Sin, Long term Illness, Death, Loss (yours or the projection of the above onto you)

*"If we say we have no sin we deceive ourselves and the truth is not in us." 1 John 1:8 KJV*

**Stage One** of the *sanctification process* is where you will look at, and hopefully identify your problem areas. These are the presenting problems of life. This is where you look at hurts, hang-ups and habits, diseases, dysfunctions, and addictions.

*A Admit Defenses Used To Cover Pain*

*I admit that I use defenses to keep you from knowing how I really feel and to cover my pain. I am not completely honest and authentic about my feelings.*

*RECOGNIZING THE OUTWARD SIGNS (defenses, the masks I wear)*

Denial, Rapid Speech, Anger, Fidgeting, Laughing, Side-ways Anger, Busy, Withdrawal, Isolation, Delusion, Distracting, Blame Frame, Labeling, Name Calling, Mind Games, Rationalize and Justify, Generalizations, Coarse Gesturing, Sarcasm, Manipulation

> *"But I tell you, on the day of Judgment men will have to give account for every idle (inoperative, non-working) word they speak. "*
> *"For by your words you will be justified and acquitted, and by your words you will be condemned and sentenced." Matthew 12:36, 37 AMP*

> *"The truth shall set you free" John 8:32 KJV*

> *"Death and life are in the power of the tongue; and they that love it shall eat the fruit thereof." Proverbs 18:21 KJV*

**Stage Two** of the model is the point in the process of *sanctification* where you identify the outward signs that come with your hurts, hang-ups, habits, life problems, diseases and dysfunctions. At this stage of the discovery process, you look at the things that you do to cover your true feelings. These are the masks that you wear your public self.

# *N* *Notice Overwhelming Feelings/Thoughts*

*I admit that my feelings and thoughts sometimes overwhelm me. My thoughts and feelings are not what they should be.*

*OVERCOMING YOUR FEELINGS (feelings, emotions, body sensations: grounded and ungrounded)*

FEELINGS (UNGROUNDED): Whenever the feeling is bigger than the event, it is ALWAYS about your history and memories about people, places or things out of your conscious awareness.

> *"The heart is deceptive above all things, and desperately wicked: who can know it?"*
> *Jeremiah 17:9 KJV*

> *"Keep thy heart with all diligence; for out of it are the issues of life." Proverbs 4:23 KJV*

> *"There is a way which seemeth right unto a man, but the end thereof are the ways of death." Proverbs 14: 12 KJV*

**Stage Three** is the point in *sanctification* where you learn to identify and overcome your uncomfortable feelings. These are the feelings that you have not allowed to come to the surface for fear of exposure. You have spent years learning to keep them hidden.

# *C* *Core Issues: Trauma/Abuse*

*I admit my core issue and face the truth of my history.*

*DEALING WITH THE REAL ISSUES (Core issues that drive my behavior, thoughts and feelings)*

Experiencing physical abuse, sexual abuse, intellectual abuse, emotional abuse, neglect, abandonment, spiritual trauma, physical trauma, medical trauma, death or extreme loss, long term illness, and/or observing the above results in: roots of bitterness, disobedience to God's commands, lies, false beliefs, and un-forgiveness causing strongholds, besetting sins, diseases, and addictions. All abuse opens the door to Satan and demonic influences.

> *"Never the less I tell you the truth. It is to your advantage that I go away; for if I do not go away, the Helper will not come to you; but if I depart, I will send Him to you."*

> *"However, when He, the Spirit of Truth has come, He will guide you into all truth; for He will not speak on His own authority, but whatever He hears He will speak; and He will tell you things to come." John 16: 7 -13 NKJV*

> *"If any of you lacks wisdom, let him ask of God, who gives to all liberally and without reproach, and it will be given to him." James 1: 5 NKJV*

**Stage Four** is where you learn to deal with the real issues of life. These are the root or core issues that are at the bottom of the pain in your life. This stage of the *sanctification* process takes you to the bottom of the issues identified in stage one: The deepest levels of the *sanctification* process are reached at this stage of the process. Failure to reach these deeper levels can be one of the contributing causes of relapse and return to the destructive behavior identified in stage one of the journey. This is a crucial stage in the process and there is need for much encouragement and support.

We believe failure to reach this stage is the cause of many relapses. This is the stage that separates the men from the boys, the women from the girls, and the spiritually mature from the *"babes in Christ."*

# *T* *Thoughts and Feelings Grounded In Reality*

*I admit my thoughts and feelings and examine them in the light of God's word.*

*WINNING OVER YOUR PAST: (The cycle of shame and guilt)*

SHAME /GUILT: Delusion, Denial, Anger, Bargaining, Sadness, Acceptance

**Shame** is about who you are. It is always about abuse, and it causes you to believe lies about who you are contrary to Scripture. **Guilt** is about what you have done. It is important to *distinguish who you are from what you have done. Separate the person from the behavior.* The Bible teaches that Christ loves the sinner and hates the sin. God turns his back on the sin; the sinner He promises to never leave nor forsake.

> *"And hope maketh not ashamed; because the love of God is shed abroad in our hearts by the Holy Ghost which is given unto you." Romans 5: 5 KJV*

*'If we confess our sins, He is faithful and just to forgive us our sins and to cleanse us from all unrighteousness." 1 John 1: 9 NKJV*

**Stage Five** is the point in the *sanctification* process where you win over the issues of the past and get freedom from your bondage.

# *I* *Identify Pain: The Grieving Process*

*I admit my pain and accept healing by grieving my losses.*

*UNDERSTANDING YOUR PAIN (The grieving process)*

GRIEVING: Grounded Feelings: The feelings of anger, sadness, fear, joy, and acceptance are now connected to the core issues. It is important to acknowledge the thoughts and feelings connected to core issues and the ways that you have suffered and your life has been affected. It is at this stage that the forgiveness work must be done.

*"Keep and guard your heart with all vigilance and above all that you guard, for out of it flow the springs of life." Proverbs 4:23 AMP*

*"But if ye forgive not men their trespasses, neither will your father forgive your trespasses." Matthew 6:15 KJV*

**Stage Six** is where you learn to understand the pain in your life. This is the point of transformation or *sanctification* of specific areas of pain and dysfunction. This is where you watch the Lord turn your scars to stars. You learn to identify your pain and connect the feelings and thoughts that go with it.

# F *Freedom to Live the Abundant Life*

*I accept my freedom as a gift from God.*

## LIVING THE VICTORIOUS LIFE IN CHRIST

*Sanctification* in the areas of brokenness: Becoming the person Christ created you to be. (Progress not perfection until the day of Christ Jesus): creative, spontaneous, alive, accountable, joyful, child-like, self actualized, life purpose discovered, displays of unconditional love.

*"The Spirit of the Lord is upon me, because he hath anointed me to preach the gospel to the poor; he hath sent me to heal the broken hearted, to preach deliverance to the captives, and recovering of sight to the blind, to set at liberty them that are bruised." Luke 4:18 KJV*

*"And he speaking began to say unto them, this day is the scripture fulfilled in your ears." Luke 4:21 KJV (Jesus speaking)*

*"Let this mind be in you, which was also in Christ Jesus." Philippians 2:5 KJV*

*"This book of the law shall not depart out of thy mouth: but thou shall meditate therein day and night, that thou mayest observe to do according to all that is written therein: for then thou shalt make thy way prosperous, and then thou shalt have good success." Joshua 1: 8 KJV*

**Stage Seven** of the *sanctification* process is where you learn how Christ sets the captives free. It is here on your journey that you discover the victorious life Christ died to give you. You truly start to live the abundant life.

*Y* *Your Story...Your Testimony of Freedom in Christ: The Sanctified Area(s) of Your Life.*

*I accept my story and my responsibility to share my testimony with others.*

The seven stages are completed and the resulting transformation becomes your story, your testimony and your new found freedom in Christ. Each time you have a problem; you can go to the model and allow the Lord to sanctify you in another area of your life. From glory to glory becoming more like Christ, less like the world, as the Lord transforms you into the creature you were meant to become.

**YOUR STORY...YOUR TESTIMONY...YOUR MISSION**

The freedom in Christ to live the "abundant life" He died to give you.

This process is never complete. You are never completely transformed until Christ comes to take you home. When applied to each area of your brokenness, you find more freedom in Christ to live the "abundant life" He died to give you. Each area of *sanctification* becomes your story...your testimony...your mission of the power of the risen, living Christ in your life.

The preceding model is designed to allow maturity in Christ for Christian(s) as you apply the seven stages to the areas of your life that you want Christ to transform. Submitting to the process invites Christ into areas of your life that look more like the world than Christ. Those seeking Christian maturity can look at their lives, look at the areas where Christ is at work and join Him there.

# DEDICATION

W e dedicate *"STOP THE VIOLENCE..." Claim the Promises of Christ©* to our fellow Christian travelers who wish to grow and mature in Christ, to the Pastors of all churches that wish to shepherd their flocks by example, growth in Christ, and discipleship training; to Christian counselors and their clients, to the many organizations that see Christ as the head of their families and businesses, wishing to glorify their maker in all that they do. To Him who is able to do exceedingly more than we could dream or imagine...To God be the glory.

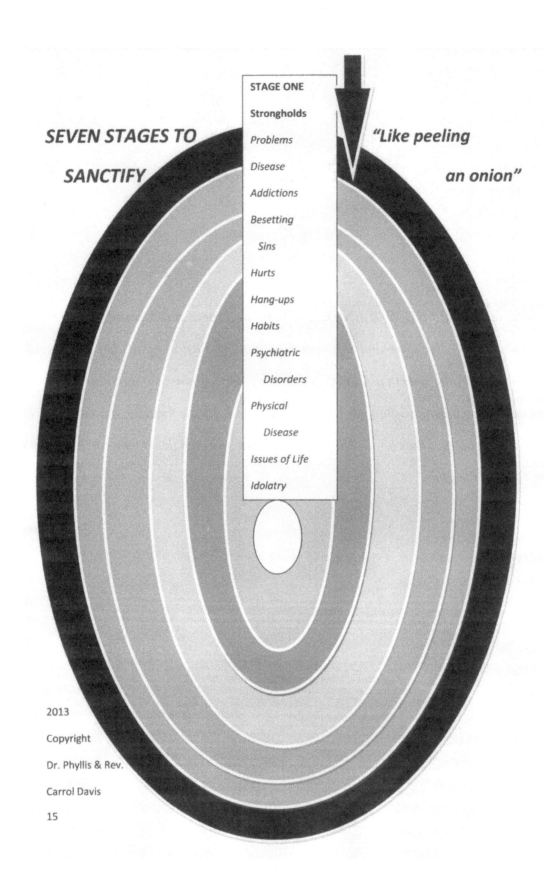

SEVEN STAGES TO SANCTIFY

"Like peeling an onion"

STAGE ONE

**Strongholds**

*Problems*

*Disease*

*Addictions*

*Besetting Sins*

*Hurts*

*Hang-ups*

*Habits*

*Psychiatric Disorders*

*Physical Disease*

*Issues of Life*

*Idolatry*

2013

Copyright

Dr. Phyllis & Rev.

Carrol Davis

15

**STOP THE VIOLENCE...SEVEN STAGES TO SANCTIFY....**
**"Like peeling an onion"**

# Section 1:

# Stage One:

# IDENTIFYING THE PROBLEM

*"Let this mind be in you which is also in Christ Jesus." Philippians 2:5*

*S* *Strongholds / Besetting Sins / Problem State*

*I* *admit that there are strongholds, besetting sins or problems that I would like healed. There are areas of my life that do not look like Christ.*

Recovery is a transformation process. The Scriptures refer to it as *sanctification*. It is not instantaneous but, progressive. You are growing in Christ in the transformation process to become more like Him. You will never reach completion until Christ comes to take you home. With Christ all things are possible. However, Christ usually uses the sins of this world and the sanctification process to develop and mature you. He can change you totally, even instantly, but usually, the change is over time.

The sanctification process starts with a new attitude as you grow into the mind of Christ. (Romans 12:12) Let the mind of Christ guide you and He will fulfill the desires of your heart. He will either give you what you desire or He will change your *"heart of stone"* to a *"heart of flesh,"* desiring only His will for your lives. (Ezekiel 36:26)

A person or child of God is one of honor and integrity. (1 Corinthians 9: 6-11). As you grow and mature in Christ you become more like Him. As you spend more time in His word, you grow and learn to apply His word to your life. As you take all of your problems and concerns to Him, He becomes more a part of your life. Christ cares about everything in life that concerns you. If it is a problem for you, it is for Him as well. It does not have to be a "spiritual" issue to take it to Christ. You are taught in Scripture to pray without ceasing and to pray about everything, making your needs known, *"be careful for nothing; but in everything by prayer and supplication with thanksgiving let your requests be made known unto God. And the peace of God, which passeth all understanding, shall keep your hearts and minds through Christ Jesus." Philippians 4:6, 7 KJV*

*"Call to me and I will answer by revealing what is hard and hidden, what you do not know" Jeremiah 33: 3 KJV.* Christ does not say just "spiritual things" or "things of God." He does not limit His revelation to you. He says He will answer your hard and hidden questions and things that you do not know. Only when you start to turn to Him with everything that concerns you, can you truly experience God and the intimacy that comes in relationship with Him. Until you learn to live and breathe the Scriptures, they are just words on a page, a nice story, a history lesson.

*"Commit to the Lord whatever you do, and your plans will succeed." Proverbs.16:3 KJV* God instructs you to commit all you think and do to Him. He does not say to go to Him with the plans you have designed and He will bless them. He tells you to commit all to Him and your plans will succeed. You are not in control. It is just an illusion, if you think that you are. The God of the universe is in control and will complete his plans, with or without your co-operation. It has been said in the *sanctification* process circles, "you can go dancing and singing or kicking and screaming." The choice of how you go is up to you.

*"Every good and perfect gift is from above, coming down from the Father of lights, with whom there is no variation or shifting shadow." James 1:17 KJV* God does not change, He has no favorites. What He does for one, He will do for all that ask and are willing. Just as you have to receive the "free" gift of salvation, you also must receive the "free gifts" of guidance and instruction. Both require something of you.....
*COMMITMENT and BELIEF.* Walking down the aisle and saying that you believe does not save you. God judges the motives of your heart. Equally true, just saying, teaching, or believing God's word does not *sanctify* you. *It is an action verb...SANCTIFY.* It is a process that requires action on your part just as being saved requires turning over your life and will to the Lord.

*"He counts the number of the stars; He calls them all by name. Great is our Lord and mighty in power. His understanding is infinite." Psalms 147:4 KJV* God knows everything that has ever happened. He knows what happened to you. He knows why you have problems in your life. He knows the solution. He knows the process. God is a gentleman. He is not going to knock down the door of your heart and come in uninvited. You must invite Him into the process.

*"God is our refuge and strength, an ever-present help in trouble. Therefore, we will not fear! "Psalms 46:1, 2 KJV* Sometimes your journey is scary. Sometimes you are afraid of people, situations and things over which you have no control. Sometimes you are afraid and don't even know why.

*"Now to Him who is able to do immeasurably beyond all we ask or imagine, be all glory forever and ever!" Ephesians 3:20 KJV* As you begin your "journey of the soul," call on the God of Power, your Friend, "Abba Father" to walk with you and He will. He will reveal the things you do not know and give you the strength to continue the journey. He will supply your every need. He will see you through to the end of your journey until He comes to take you home.

### *Purpose*

Your body does not belong to you it belongs to God. (1 Corinthians 6:19, 20 KJV) You were bought with a price the perfect sacrifice, Jesus Christ and you were saved to glorify your maker. It is your responsibility to guard God's temple. The gifts God gives you are to glorify Him, for building up the body of Christ. (1 Peter 4) As you grow in your transformation and the *sanctification* process, you will have more testimonies to share. You will have more intimate moments with your Savior to share how the Scriptures have come alive in your life and how the Lord has provided and protected. He will gift you with a heart for His people and a desire to share your Savior and Friend.

Listed below is a more exhaustive list to help you identify the area of *sanctification* that you would like to see the Lord transform.

Circle any area where the Holy Spirit seems to be working and calling to your attention.

**IDOLATRY:** Any time people, places or things take the place in your lives that is designed for God you are practicing idolatry:

Football          Soccer          Baseball          Basketball          Tennis          Golf          Boating

Shopping          Dancing          Exercising          Television          Computers          Fishing          Hunting

Motocross          Hang-gliding          Parasail          Addiction to Adrenalin Rush

**HURTS/HABITS/HANG-UPS:** Any time a behavior hurts you or others, becomes destructive to your relationship with God or others you may be experiencing:

Procrastination          Constantly Late          Constantly Early          Gossip          Tale Bearing

Broken Promises          Hypocritical Actions/Behaviors          Cursing/ Foul Mouth

Alienation          Negative Self Image          Hyper-Alertness          Flashbacks / Nightmares

Exaggerating Truth/ Lying          Nail Biting          Hair Pulling          Cutting          Poor Hygiene

Fear of Rejection     Fear of Anger     Isolation     Fear of Being Alone          Problems Sleeping

**PROBLEMS/LIFE EXPERIENCES**: Many times the problems of life over which you have no control can create stress and throw you into distress, the problem(s) might be:

Divorce/ Separation     Chronic Illness     Loss of a Loved One     Death

Relationship Issues     Marital Problems     Parenting Problems     Care-Giver Problems

Loss of a Friend / Loss of a Pet     Loss of a Job     Financial Burdens     Legal Problems

Loss of Interest in Work or Activities     Problems with Intimate Relationships

Difficulty with Authority Figures     Emotional Distance from Wife/Children

Problems at Work     Pride     False Humility     Volunteering     Laziness     Busyness/Driven

Self Centered     Perfectionist     Anger Issues

**SIN/DISOBEDIENCE TO GOD'S LAWS & COMMANDS:** Any time you break God's laws, commandments and are disobedient you are in need of forgiveness, reconciliation, and turning your lives around. Your history may include:

Womanizing    Adultery    Fornication    Rape    Incest Sodomy    Robbery    Greed    Murder

Slander    Gossip    Drunkenness    Gluttony    Strife    Parental Disobedience

Tale Bearing    False Witness    Murder    Witchcraft    Sorcery    Envy    Homosexual

Un-forgiveness    Strife    Believing Lies    Roots of Bitterness    Liars

Foul Mouth Reviler    Extortion    Cheat    Bestiality    Swindler    Sex with the dead

Lasciviousness    Variance    Wrath    Envy    Impure    Immoral

Unclean    Seditions    Hate    Emulations    Heresies    Magic Arts    Horoscopes

Palm Reading    Channeling    Séance    Astral Projection    Table Lifting

Fortune Telling    Astrology    Some Video Games    Crystals or Pyramids

Ouija Board    Automatic Writing    Tarot Cards    Spirit Guides    Blood Pact    Magic 8 Ball

Idolatry: Worship of the Gods of Money, Power, Position, Material Things, People, Status

The pride of life: I am the best teacher, preacher, accountant, salesman, student, mechanic, etc. I am irreplaceable. I am the most handsome, prettiest, most skilled, etc.

**ADDICTIONS:** It is not when you use, what you use, or how much you use. It is what using does to you and your life that causes the use to be out of control. It can affect one area or all areas of your life: work, home, spiritual, relationships, and/ or your health. Addictions usually come in threes. Once you have identified one, you might look for the other two. Use does not have to be immoral or illegal to be addiction. Your addiction(s) might include:

Alcohol      Drugs      Prescription Meds      Street Drugs      Gambling      Sex

Relationships      Religion      Shopping      Hoarding      Pornography      Love Addiction

Co-dependency      Electronic Gadgets      Work a holism      Sugar      Carbohydrates      Caffeine

Exercise      Food      Jewelry      Shoes      Clothes      Womanizing      Sports

**\*PHYSICAL DISEASES:** Physical problems must first be treated by a medical doctor. Many times addressing the underlying issues resolves physical manifestations of those issues. I have personally witnessed the phenomena in the following areas:

Migraine Headaches      Muscle Disorders      Chronic Pain      Vision Problems      Backaches

Cancer      Heart Disease      Broken Bones      Fibromyalgia      Blindness

Restless Leg Syndrome      Irritable Bowel Syndrome      Stomach Problems      Crones      Arthritis

High/Low Blood Pressure      Panic Attacks      Somatic Pain      Memory Impairment      Obesity

**PSYCHIATRIC DISORDERS** can manifest in the above forms of physical symptoms as well as the psychiatric diagnosis. The following is a partial list from the diagnostic manual of psychiatric disorders. The model has been successfully applied to most all of the psychiatric disorders listed with the exception of Sociopathic Disorders. While helpful, the success with this patient population is still unknown. These disorders are:

Depression          Anxiety          Anorexia          Bulimia          Thin/Fat Disorder          Phobias

Panic Attacks          Obsessive/Compulsive Disorders          Dissociative Disorder          Seizures

Gender Identity Disorder          Dissociative Identity Disorder          Eating Disorder          Manic-Depressive

Bi Polar Disorder          Conduct Disorder          Borderline Personality Disorder          MPD

Sleep Disorders          Thought Disorders          Addictions          Schizoaffective Disorder

Paranoia          Social Phobias and Fears          Pyromania          Multiple Sclerosis          Schizophrenia

Cynicism          Anger Issues          Psychic/Emotional Numbing          Survivor Guilt

Conduct Disorder          Suicidal Thoughts          Post Traumatic Stress Disorders

If the Holy Spirit has brought something to your mind that is not listed above, add it here:

_____

In the above examples your life is out of control if focused on any of the above and you hear complaints from family, friends and associates about time, attention, focus and money associated with any of the above. God is not at the center. Your priorities are out of order. Your life is out of balance. You neglect areas of your life that need and deserve your attention.

*Physical diseases such as muscle disease(s), heart disease(s) and cancer(s) have also been linked to deeper psychological and spiritual issues. We have personally witnessed physical problems solved using this model to address the underlying issues. Patients with multiple sclerosis, migraine headache(s), fibromyalgia, back pain, stomach problems and poor eye sight have improved or experienced a complete healing, using the model for the *sanctification* process.

When you start on the "journey of the soul......the *sanctification* process," God promises to continue the good work in you until it is completed.

*"The one who began a good work in you will carry it on until it is completed." Philippians 1:6 KJV*

### Do Not Forsake the Company of One Another

One of the most effective lies of the enemy is that we can continue in friendship and association with those that are not of Christ and have no interest in His ways. We are to depart from the ways of Satan and the people that practice them and to associate with fellow followers of Christ. (1 Corinthians 15:33, 34)

Association and evangelism are two different categories. We are still to take the promise of the gospel and its message to all. Relationships seek the lowest level. If we associate with those that are not Christians, they will pull us down to their level, not the reverse. *"Be not deceived: evil communications corrupt good manners. Awake to righteousness, and sin not; for some have not the knowledge of God: I speak this to your shame." 1 Corinthians 15:33, 34*

Scripture teaches us to avoid certain acts and the people that practice them. Obeying God's word will help you stay focused on the healing process.

*Revelation 21:8 KJV: "But the cowardly, the unbelieving, the vile, the murderers, the sexually immoral, those who practice magic arts, the idolaters and all liars-their place will be in the fiery lake of burning sulfur. This is the second death."*

*Galatians 5:19-21 KJV: "Now the works of the flesh are manifest, which are these, adultery, fornication, uncleanness, lasciviousness, idolatry, witchcraft\*(\* drugs, sorcery, see notes on Greek-English Lexicon) , hatred, variance, emulations, wrath, strife, seditions, heresies, envying, murders, drunkenness, revellings, and such like: of the which I tell you before, as I have also told you in time past, that they which do such things shall not inherit the kingdom of God."*

*1 Corinthians 6: 9, 10 AMP: "Do you not know that the unrighteous and the wrongdoers will not inherit or have any share in the kingdom of God? Do not be deceived (misled) neither the impure and immoral, nor idolaters, nor adulterers, nor those who participate in homosexuality, nor cheats (swindlers and thieves), nor greedy graspers, nor drunkards, nor foul mouth revilers, and slanderers, nor extortionist and robbers will inherit or have any share in the kingdom of God." "Such some of you were (once) but you were washed clean (purified by complete atonement for sin and made free from the guilt of sin) and you were consecrated (set apart, hallowed) and you were justified (pronounced righteous by trusting in the name of the Lord Jesus Christ and in the (Holy) Spirit of our God."*

Notice that the word of God teaches you the people and behaviors to avoid without allowance for their relationship to you. Many times you will be called on to leave mother, father, sister, brother, *son, *daughter, husband, or wife for the cause of Christ. You are taught in the process to leave peers, friends, circumstances, places, things, even children that refuse to obey the word of God. (*Son and *daughter as referenced above refer to grown children)

Review your list of associations and circle the people from your present and your past that need to be avoided. Move these people out of your list of close friends and associates and move them to your prayer list.

## *FAMILY MEMBERS*

Mother          Father                Stepmother              Stepfather

Grandmother (maternal)          Grandfather (maternal)              Grandmother (paternal)

Grandfather (paternal)          Brother(s)          Sisters(s)          Brother In-law          Sister In-law

Son(s) Daughter(s)          Step-son(s)              Step-daughter(s)          Granddaughter(s)

Grandson(s)          Daughter In-law          Son In-law

## *BUSINESS*

Partners          Associates          Clients          Customers          Employees

Service Providers          CPA              Suppliers          Bankers          Accountants

Insurance Agent(s)          Mechanic          Dentist          Doctors          Therapist

## *FRIENDS*

Neighbors          Bowling league          Sports fans          Exercise Buddy          Hobby Partner

Golf Buddy          Musicians          Dance partner(s)          Bingo friends          School associates

Church friends          Pastor          Counselor          Sunday school leader/teacher          School teacher(s)

**Prayer List**: Listed below are the people that I need to take off my list of close association(s) and move to my prayer list. They do not exhibit the character traits of the fruit of the spirit and are choosing a path different than the one God has called me to.

| | |
|---|---|
| 1._____ | 7._____ |
| 2._____ | 8._____ |
| 3._____ | 9._____ |
| 4._____ | 10._____ |
| 5._____ | 11._____ |
| 6._____ | 12._____ |

## Prayer

*Heavenly Father, give me wisdom and discernment when choosing friends, relationships, and business associates. Let me live according to your word to be equally yoked. Father lead me to the friendships and associations of your choosing and set me on the path of righteousness for your name sake. Give me the strength I need to turn away from any association that does not support my new commitment to sanctification and growth. Give me the courage to leave behind the people, places, and things that have supported my areas of brokenness. I turn away from these people, places, things, and turn to you Jesus, the author and finisher of our faith. I lift up_____, _____, _____, and _____ to you. I ask that you draw them to you with loving kindness, give them what they need, not necessarily what they want, so that they can bring their cracked pots and broken vessels to you for healing, surrendering that area of their life that looks more like the world than Christ. It is in your Son's precious name, Jesus that I pray.*

*Amen*

*Make a commitment to pray for these people for a minimum of thirty days and or until God releases you.*

While on the journey, choose others that are also on the journey to accompany you. You need like minded individuals who are sold out to God, people that will tell you the truth of the word and your life as the Scriptures apply. *"Not forsaking the assembling of ourselves together..."Hebrews 10:25*

We all need accountability persons in our lives. Think through the list of friends and associates above. Make a new list of persons that are walking in the process of *sanctification* and choose one to be your accountability person. This is a person that you commit to call, meet with, pray with, and involve in your process. This is someone that you know does not have your particular issue to work on. They have submitted that area of their life to Christ and have been healed. This person needs to be someone farther along than you are, if at all possible, and someone of the same sex. Pray and ask the Lord Jesus to pick the best accountability person for you and when He answers, be swift to follow His leading. *"Iron sharpeneth iron; so a man sharpeneth the countenance of his friend." Proverbs 27:17*

**Prayer**

*Heavenly Father, Holy Spirit I ask for your wisdom and discernment in asking someone to be my accountability partner, prayer warrior. I ask that over the next couple of days and weeks you bring this person to my mind, heart and spirit. Impress upon me the person of your choice. Open my ears to hear your gentle leading. Give me the strength and courage to follow through on the decision your spirit leads me to make. I ask you to speak to this person, just as you have spoken to me. Put on their heart a spirit of receptiveness to my request, confirm the choice you have made for me. It is the name of Jesus that I pray. Amen.*

**Exercise: Accountability**

Break up into groups of two males with males, females with females. We will call one person A and the other person B. People in group A will put on the blind folds. The people in group B are the guides. The people in group B are not to touch the people in group A, unless A is in danger of walking into a wall, chair, or object that might harm them, etc. Person B's job is to protect person A as they do the exercise. Person B must put their body in front of person A to prevent person A from running into a wall, chair etc. Person B is to guide the hand of person A away from the face of another person. Group A reaches out to touch another person from the group. The first person that a member from group A touches is their new accountability partner.

Now person B puts on the blind fold and the roles are reversed. Person A serves as a guide to protect person B as person B does the exercise. The first person that B touches will be their new accountability partner.

For the next couple of days and weeks the people from group A and group B will call the first person they touched their new accountability partner. This person will remain your accountability partner until the Lord chooses someone else for you. Go stand by that person now and exchange telephone numbers. Set up boundaries around when it is OK to touch base with each other. You have five minutes. In the event you feel led by the Lord to ask someone else to be your dialogue partner, please notify one of the trainers so that your current partner can be reassigned.

Accountability means you commit to the following areas:
1. Pray for each other and the area you are asking the Lord to "sanctify."
2. Help each other learn and practice the things we are learning outside of session.
3. Read from the Scriptures one chapter every day.
4. Openly discuss any areas that are challenging for you sharing your experiences. Discuss your thoughts and feelings.
5. Agree to inform a trainer of any area of concern that you were unable to resolve at the next session.
6. In an emergency situation, if your partner will not call, you call and report the problem.

If there is anyone that is unwilling or unable to participate, and/or anyone that has questions about this exercise, ask for assistance by raising your hand.

**Exercise: Boundaries, "Safe" and "Unsafe" People**

Now break up into groups of three. Give each person a chance to talk about their experience. Answer the following questions:

1. Was it easy for you to trust your guide when you were blindfolded? Why? Or Why not?

2. Was it hard for you to trust your guide when you were blindfolded? Why? Or Why not?

3. Did you know this person prior to this exercise? How well did you know them?

4. How is this reflective of the boundaries in your life? Do you know what a boundary is?

5. Do you have boundaries that are walled off? Are your relationships enmeshed?

6. Are your boundaries broken or not even there physically? What about emotionally? Do you have spiritual boundaries? Talk about your intellectual and sexual boundaries.

7. Do you know the difference between "safe" and "unsafe" people? Do you have different boundaries for different associations?

8. Do you share different things and experiences with these different associations? Do you share equally?

Think about the example set for us by Jesus Christ, the only perfect God/man. He had strong boundaries around His spiritual beliefs and the teachings of the Gospel. He would not be swayed nor tricked by the Pharisees. He had a close association with James, John, and Peter. They were in His inner circle. He met thousands of people at the feeding of the multitudes, he loved all. All people did not know Him the same way. This is what we are referring to as "boundaries."

## ADDICTIONS

It has been our experience that addictions usually run in threes. If you have identified one major addiction, problem, or besetting sin; be alert for the second and third problems. If you are not careful to go inward toward resolution, you stand in danger of trading one problem state for another, *cross addiction*. The idea is to move toward the center to the core issues, much like peeling an onion. It is not unusual to have a person that is addicted to alcohol to also be addicted to drugs. Denial, refusal to believe the truth of a matter, is common in all addictions. A person may admit to drinking alcohol, but refuses to believe it is a problem in their life. It is not unusual to have a person confirm their addiction to beer while believing they can safely switch to vodka or whiskey. The biological makeup of an addict's body, their psychological health, and the sociological influences of their life make them prime candidates for addiction to any substance abuse, including aspirin. The substance does not have to produce a "high" to be an addiction. The definition of addiction is that the use of the addicted "person, place, or thing" causes a person to be unable to function in one area of their life: work or school, home, or relationships. Use does not have to be illegal or immoral to be an addiction.

In order to be brief, most of the references are to drugs and/or alcohol. The same principles apply to all drugs of choice, besetting sin, problem state, acting out behavior including, but not limited to eating disorders: thin/fat disorder, bulimia, anorexia; all addictions: gambling, alcohol, drugs, sex, pornography, work a holic; some psychiatric diseases: obsessive, compulsive disorders, chronic pain, depression, identity disorder; some physical diseases: muscle diseases, hearing loss, vision problems, and most always besetting sin, and problems such as procrastination, lying, etc. (See stage one problem state: hurts, hang-ups, and habits).

Addicts also minimize their use and usually report using much less than they actually do. The disease also blinds the addict to the consequences of their use. They cannot seem to connect the dots between their uses, the destructive cycle in their life, and the loss of friends, family, jobs, opportunities, and finances. If they do not receive help in the early stage(s) of addiction, they will constitute a large majority of the homeless population of a city. Many people and most Christians do not understand the disease and think that the person is truly down on their luck and just in need of a little assistance, which they offer in the form of a place to stay, food, shelter, clothing, and money. We refer to this as enabling.

**ENABLING**

Sometimes church members believe the addict just needs to be saved and their problems will be solved. They offer the addict a tool to manipulate, by offering salvation as a way out. The addict says a prayer, walks the aisle, and the church becomes the addicts' number one *"supporter."* They do not understand that this kind of help keeps the person stuck and prevents them from facing the pain of their addiction and seeking real help. Recovery circles call this kind of help *"enabling behavior."* Some churches are starting to wake up and understand that this kind of assistance is not only unhelpful; but rather, is deadly to the addict. Some of the more progressive churches are labeling this kind of help as "Toxic Charity."

An enabler is one who prevents the addict from experiencing the natural consequences of his/her behavior, in order for the reality of the disease and its consequences to be faced breaking through the addicts' denial. Only then can they admit their problem and seek real help and the *sanctification* process.

***Common characteristics of enablers are:*** They accept lies for the truth, allow themselves to be exploited, misled and outsmarted. They threaten, preach, lecture, nag, manipulate, and argue with the addict. They lose their temper, postpone plans, and make excuses for the addict. They drink and or use with them one time and throw the alcohol or pills down the drain the next time. They cover up for the addicts' misbehavior and withdraw. None of these things work to control addiction. The enabler did not cause the addiction and can not cure it. Only the addict can do that.

The enabler continues to blame others, accept blame, resist change, bails the addict out of jail one more time, gives the addict one more chance, lends money, extracts promises, undermines others, acts as a buffer to the consequences of use, uses emotional appeal or blackmail, is super responsible, does not talk about the problem, ignores the addict's use and is defensive. All of these negative behaviors send the enablers life into a destructive cycle of its own without intervention.

When enablers shield the addict from the consequences of their behaviors, actions and attitudes, they are killing them with kindness, minimizing the addicts' behavior while accepting responsibility for them. *Doing for someone what they can, and should be doing for themselves, keeps the addict stuck in denial and the enabler spinning down the drain of self destruction.* Some common examples of enabling behavior are: giving or lending money, cars, and rides; paying their bills, court costs, child support, or rent. The only help that is really loving is support to treat the disease: rehabilitation for the drug of choice, 12 step programs, Celebrate Recovery (Christian based 12 step programs), in-patient treatment for a minimum of thirty days, outpatient individual and group therapy with therapist trained in substance abuse, dual diagnosis, and family systems work. (Most medical doctors, psychiatrists, and some psychologist, counselors, and pastors are not trained in these fields, and can do more harm than good assisting the addict with a new addiction to prescription medication and more problems than before).

Why do enablers do these destructive things? Many of them think that their behavior is the Christian thing to do. They do not understand addiction and do not rightly apply the word of God to the situation. They are usually caring, concerned people with a lack of awareness, information, knowledge, and skills. Sometimes they act out of guilt, fear, or in an effort to protect. Sometimes the addict plays on the enabler's fears and failures to manipulate the rescue they desire. Sometimes the enabler does not want the addict to get better for fear of losing them or losing control.

Enablers feel responsible for others; not accountability to others. They are manipulators that put their expectations on others. They try to fix, protect, rescue and control. They are concerned with the solution, the answers, and are concerned that the details are correct, that they are right, and that they do the right thing in all circumstances. They carry their feelings and don't usually listen. They believe that if they can just find the right combination of solutions, and circumstances, they can fix, rescue and cure the addict. They must hear over and over again that they did not cause the disease and that they cannot cure it. That is up to the addict.

Enablers either get into the *sanctification* process to correct their dysfunctional behavior and start on their own journey and *sanctification* process or fall into a life of destruction, cycling downward alongside the addict. Enabling can lead to its own addiction, depression, anxiety or disease cycle. At the end of their journey with the addict they are emotionally, physically, spiritually and sometimes economically bankrupt. They are anxious, fearful, tired and feel used up.

### *Progressive and Chronic Disease State*

If one has been in the *sanctification* process and has abstained from use for a long period of time, one slip and one time of use, can throw the recovering addict into a downward cycle. It will be worse than the last time, within three months of continued use. Scripture talks about the parable of the man that was possessed by demons, the house being swept clean of the demons, and if not replaced the demons will return seven times worse than before:

*"When the unclean spirit is gone out of a man, he walketh through dry places, seeking rest, and findeth none. Then he saith, I will return into my house from which I came out; and when he is come, he findeth it empty, swept and garnished. Then goeth he, and taketh with himself seven other spirits more wicked than himself, and they enter in and dwell there: and the last state of that man is worse than the first." Matthew 12:43-45a KJV.*

This is a true picture of addiction and all besetting sins, the progression, and chronic nature. Alcoholism and drug addiction can be arrested...not cured. There is a term in the recovery field called a "dry drunk" meaning a person who has stopped using the chemicals and drug of choice yet has not submitted to the *sanctification* process. Christ has not been given access to all areas of the "dry drunk's" life, and his life has not changed except for the fact that he/she no longer ingests the "drug of choice."

"Progression," as referred to in the chart below speaks of alcoholism, substitute *"alcohol"* with your *"drug of choice"*( E.g.: people, places, things, drugs, street drugs, gambling, pornography, sex, food, shopping, golf, football, baseball, tennis, soccer, dance, exercise, etc.) See the extensive list in stage one and use one of the areas that you identified for *sanctification*.

## Prayer

*Father, Holy Spirit, thank you for guiding me into all truth. Thank you for shining your light of awareness into the areas of my life that you wish to sanctify and cleanse. Thank you, Father, for allowing me to view my life through the lens of your word. Help me, Father, not to lean on my own understanding but rather to allow you to guide my process as I seek counsel and healing in my areas of brokenness. I will give you the glory Father, for all you have done and are going to do in my life. Thank you for your strength for the journey. It is in Jesus precious name that I pray.*

*Amen*

**Exercise**

*Below are the symptoms of the progression of the disease and the downward spiral. Circle any that apply to your addict with the red pen.

    ✓ Preoccupation with drinking or using, or partying. Only socialize with other users.

    ✓ Increased tolerance

    ✓ Gulps drinks or drugs

    ✓ Using alone

    ✓ Use as a medicine

    ✓ Blackouts (Amnesia) or Brown Outs (Don't remember what you did).

    ✓ Hidden bottles, stash or usage

    ✓ Non-premeditated drinking or using

    ✓ Morning tremors, sweats, or butterflies

    ✓ Morning use to get going

    ✓ Change in friends

    ✓ Change or deterioration of places frequented

    ✓ Lack of motivation

    ✓ Change in eating habits

    ✓ Change in sleeping patterns

    ✓ Isolation from family

    ✓ Distorted thinking/ inability to concentrate

    ✓ Time missed from school or work

    ✓ Lying (calling in sick to work or school, making up stories to account for time lost)

    ✓ Abrupt mood swings, lethargic and defensive; Violent behavior towards friends / family

    ✓ Dropped performance at school or work

    ✓ Decreased interest in hobbies and activities

✓ Physical deterioration: weight loss, weight gain, loss of color, circles under the eyes, glassy eyes, trance, bulbous nose, red eyes, dilated or constricted pupils, loss of co-ordination.

✓ Memory loss (Can't find your way home....your car...take taxis...bus, etc).

✓ Cross- Addiction: Changing drug of choice to solve problems i.e. bourbon to beer to wine to pills, marijuana

✓ Compare use with others to minimize or deny the problem or addictive nature of use

✓ Rationalize and justify use with the fact that the doctor prescribed the "drug of choice" i.e. wine, beer, alcohol, sex, pills, sexual behavior

(See illustration Progression of the Disease)


**Exercise**

Now go back to the above check list and circle any that apply to you and your process with the blue pen. Notice that the progression of the disease in your addict has progressed in your own enabling behaviors.

Addiction(s), besetting sin(s), hurts, habits, hang-ups, psychiatric disease, problem states, disease, chronic and long term illness affect the entire family system. Every member of the system needs treatment and support.

## Onset of Disease Reflects In Family

## Without Help

- arguments
- distrust
- unhappiness
- religious needs
- denial (fantasy)
- problems multiply
- threats made-not carried out
- blues
- intolerance
- suspicion
- worry
- irritability

- burdened by responsibility
- loss of interest
- imaginary illnesses
- facade
- uses prescription drugs
- loss of self respect
- remorse/isolation
- social withdrawal
- patent medicine use
- indefinable fears
- drug user
- bankruptcy of alibis
- escape
- infidelity/jealousy
- dishonesty
- depression
- irrational behavior
- alibis
- blames others
- self neglect/extravagance

# *Entire Family Affected by Disease and It's Progression*

Addiction is a disease, a state of besetting sin that affects the entire family system. Each member needs to find their own journey of *sanctification* and healing to be most effective. An accurate comparison of an addict on their journey of *sanctification* that returns to the untreated family is much like taking the car that has four flat tires to the shop and fixing only one tire. The results would be similar to the car with only one tire repaired.

*Dysfunctional family members take on specific roles and family scripts* to deal with the pain of the dysfunctional family. The dysfunction can be as a result of any of the stage one diseases, addictions, problem states, sins, etc. The family roles help the members survive the dysfunctional system, unhealthy as they are. Identifying the role(s) that you played in your family of origin may help to shed the light of healing on some of the dysfunctional coping characteristics you have carried into adulthood.

Originally developed for use in the treatment field of alcoholism, used here to address all stage one issues:

**Exercise: Family Roles and Coping Mechanisms**

Some of the family roles and the characteristics of each role follow. Circle the role that most resembles your ways of coping. You may have more than one role. Some people have combined roles to cope with the dysfunction in their families.

**THE HERO / THE STAR/THE PRINCESS/ THE PRINCE/DIVA**: Usually the oldest child. The family hero's role is to provide self worth for the family. The hero has a wall of defenses that covers the hero's true feelings of hurt, loneliness, confusion, inadequacy, and anger. The wall of defenses compulsively covers up the true feelings and the family hero lives in the trap of self-delusion. The world sees the wall of defenses as the real person: super responsible, successful, all-together, independent life away from the family, works hard for approval.

**THE LOST CHILD / THE FORGOTTEN / THE GOOD CHILD**: Usually the child with the most pain. The lost child's role in the family is usually relief. The family does not have to worry about this child. (Delusion) The lost child has a wall of defenses that covers the true feelings of hurt, loneliness, inadequacy, rejection, and anger. The world sees the child as distant, sometimes overweight, super-independent, withdrawn, quiet, and aloof. These are the defenses that hide the pain.

**THE MASCOT / THE CLOWN:** Sometimes the youngest child. The role is to provide the family with fun and humor. The wall of defenses that covers the mascot's pain are being super cute, fragile, humorous, and hyperactive, clowning, and doing anything to attract attention. The wall of defenses covers the pain and true feelings of insecurity, fear, confusion and loneliness. The wall of defenses keeps the mascot trapped in self delusion.

**THE SCAPEGOAT / THE PROBLEM**: Known in the "the *sanctification* process" community as the ambulance driver, the one that finally brings help to the family. The scapegoat's role is to provide distraction and focus for the family. The wall of defenses includes chemical use, unplanned pregnancy, acting out, strong peer value, withdrawn, and sullen. The wall of defenses covers the scapegoat's true feelings of rejection, anger, loneliness, hurt, fear, and defiance.

**THE CHIEF ENABLER**: The role of the chief enabler is to provide responsibility for the family. The wall of defenses includes powerlessness, self pity, super-responsibility, seriousness, self-blaming, fragility, and manipulation. The feelings that the wall of defenses protects are: anger, fear, guilt, hurt, and pain. Chief enablers live in the trap of self-delusion.

**THE ADDICT/CHRONICALLY ILL/PSYCHIATRIC DISORDER**: The role of this person is to provide focus and distraction for the dysfunction in the family. The wall of defenses includes rigidity, aggression, perfectionism, anger, charm, righteousness, and grandiosity. The wall of defenses keeps the dependent person trapped in self-delusion with feelings of fear, hurt, guilt, pain, and shame.

## Exercise

Workshop participants, breakout into your groups and take turns discussing the family roles you played in your family of origin. Talk about how these roles helped you survive. Do you still use these coping mechanisms when under stress? Do they still work or are they getting in the way of your becoming all that Christ meant for you to be? Take five minutes per person. Choose a timekeeper to keep you on track and allow time for each group member to share.

Notice that children are very creative and have used roles and coping strategies to survive. These coping strategies helped us survive impossible situations that we were never intended to have to cope with. Yet, as adults, if we do not recognize when we are falling into our old coping habits and patterns, we will miss the blessings of the abundant life Christ died to give us.

## Exercise

Tell your accountability partner what your roles were, what coping mechanisms and strategies you used to avoid pain. Ask them to call you on it when you go into coping instead of honest and congruent communication.

***Treatment goals for the whole family include***: detoxification of all members (if necessary), breaking through the wall of delusion, acceptance of the disease, sin, or problem state, and the *sanctification* process of the whole person, including recognition of thoughts and feelings. The family is encouraged to work together sharing feeling, accepting and forgiving each other, while rebuilding the family system. Possible outcomes include: The addict/chronically ill/dependent person gets well. The family gets well. Everyone get well. No one gets well. Each individual must accept responsibility for his/or her own process and journey. Members should work together to achieve their goals individually and as a family. A possible outcome is a family much stronger and healthier than before the process. Members are cautioned to HALT. Don't get too hungry, angry, lonely, or tired. If you are hungry, eat. If you are angry, talk it out or journal about your feelings. When you are lonely go to a meeting, call your sponsor or your accountability partner. If you are tired, get rest. Take care of your physical body. It is the temple of God.

Examples in this next section use alcohol as the "drug of choice" or problem state to talk about addiction. Addiction is not limited to alcohol; it encompasses all of the problem states on the model, including addictions to sex, drugs, love, relationships, gambling, prescription medication, food, pornography, shopping, sports, religion, etc. The characteristics of "sin" and "addiction" are the same and can be applied to the specific "drug of choice" that you are addressing, be it pornography, drugs, food, gambling or street drugs. Addiction is no respecter of persons, socio-economic level, race, gender or occupation. It is a disease with sin at its core, and it can and does affect anyone.

*"For all have sinned and come short of the glory of God." Romans 3:23 KJV*

### Early Intervention: Disease Can Be Arrested

*Intervention,* a situation where numerous friends, relatives, and associates confront the person on the destructive nature of their use, is one way to break through the denial at an early stage. Another effective intervention is to involve the family of the addict in the process. They are usually in a lot of pain and thus more motivated to seek change. The addict is usually numb to his or her pain, in denial, and not interested in change. Taking videos and recordings of outburst and irrational behavior can help to break the denial and delusion. As the family in the system changes, the addict is forced to change. Hopefully the change will be to seek healing.

### Co-dependent...Co-Addict

Any person, place or thing that you allow to get between you and your relationship with Christ is idolatry. Christ is to be first and foremost in your heart, mind, and spirit. You are to look to Christ to fulfill all of your needs. If you substitute any person or thing in the place Christ is meant to fulfill, you might have temporary satisfaction. Your satisfaction will be short lived. Seemingly good things can turn into idolatry when you get your priorities out of order, including your relationship with your children, your spouse, and your hobbies: golfing, boating, sports, shopping, busyness, service work, etc.

Any person that lives with, loves, or is in relationship with an addict is a co-addict and a co-dependent. These problems bring with them a set of behaviors that are dysfunctional and road blocks to becoming all that Christ meant for you to be.

Co dependency is an issue for most Christians that grew up in a dysfunctional family. The attitudes seem like those of Christian teachings on the surface. Further examination points out the false belief(s) and lies that have fueled your dysfunctional thinking and behavior. Do any of these apply to your thinking and false beliefs? Circle any of the following characteristics that apply to you.

- Co-dependents always put others first before taking care of themselves. (Aren't Christians supposed to put others first?)
- Co-dependents give themselves away. (Shouldn't Christians do the same?)
- Co-dependents martyr themselves. (Christianity honors martyrs.)
- Co-dependents fear confrontation. (Aren't Christians supposed to do so?)
- Co-dependents seek to please others. (Aren't Christians supposed to do so?)

These statements have a familiar ring, and many of you were taught these principles in the church. These are false teachings and distorted life applications of the Scriptures. How can you distinguish co-dependency from the teachings of Christ? How can you distinguish true Christian maturity from co-dependent characteristics?

Jesus taught the value of each individual when He created you and formed you in your mother's womb. Life is His gift to you to be cherished and valued. Because He first loved you, you look to Him to understand love. He said that you are to love others *equally* as yourselves, *not more than*. Christ taught us to love our neighbors as ourselves. A love of God and of self forms the basis for loving others. The difference between a life of service for God and others is the motive. The motives for service to God and others are either out of a love for God; or out of co-dependent needs. One motive *gives* out of love. The other motive *takes* out of need.

| THE LOVE OF GOD | CO-DEPENDENCY |
|---|---|
| *Gives out of love* | *Takes out of need* |
| • Desire | Fear |
| • Want to | Guilt |
| • Get to | Reaction to Outside Stimuli |
| • Approved by God | Desire for Approval of People |
| • Appointment of God | Need to Be Needed |
| • Valued as a Child of God | Value Depends on Others Approval |
| • Desire to Please God | Desire to Please People |

Motive is the key to healthy service. Healthy people are at choice, they choose to serve. As a close friends says in regard to his service for Christ, *"I get to; not I got to."* What motivates you?

God judges the heart. Works that are done with the wrong motive or out of co-dependency rather than love will be burned up. Healthy people have balanced lives, know how to order priorities and serve out of love and desire. If you would resent doing something, you should not do it, because you are doing the action for the wrong motive. The action needs to come from the correct motivation: the love of God.

**Exercise**

*Co-dependents believe lies that are from the pit of hell. Start replacing the lies with the truth about you and who you are from the word of God. Some common false beliefs follow, circle the ones that apply to you and start reprogramming your mind with God's truth.*

✓ I have little or no value.

✓ Other persons and situations have all the value.

✓ I must please other people regardless of the cost to my own person or my own values.

✓ I am to place myself to be used by others without protest. I must give myself away.

✓ If I claim any rights for myself I am selfish.

✓ I guess at what normal is.

✓ I have trouble completing projects...procrastination.

✓ I judge myself and others harshly.

✓ I don't know how to have fun.

✓ I take things too seriously.

✓ I have difficulty with intimate relationships.

✓ I constantly seek approval, affection and admiration from others.

✓ I overreact to changes over which I have no control.

✓ I am super responsible...or super irresponsible.

✓ I am extremely loyal...even if it isn't deserved.

✓ I seek immediate gratification.

✓ I am impulsive.

✓ I don't listen to wise counsel from family, friends.

Co dependents seek approval and a sense of worth outside of themselves in *external stimuli*, rather than the *internal* approval of Jesus Christ, their Lord and Savior. They characteristically take on your pain and struggle as their own, working hard to solve your problems. They do not follow Christ's model to lead and guide, allowing you to experience the consequences of your own behavior and actions. Your hobbies and interest become theirs and they link themselves to your dreams. Co-dependents only have an opinion when you approve and /or agree with them. The quality of their lives is directly linked to the quality of yours. They are not their own person. Over time they can surrender their complete identity to the other person. Most co-dependents do not even know what they like or don't like, find it hard to make decisions unless they know you approve. *Sanctification* in this area involves a process of learning and discovering who one is without the input of anyone else. Who does God say that you are? It is a process that includes discovery of ones talents, interests, hobbies, opinions, dreams, and self worth. The *sanctification* process allows co-dependents to regain their identity through Christ and they come to believe the truth about who God says they are. The process allows Christ to have direction in their life to become the creatures Christ died for them to become.

Without treatment co-dependent beliefs are reflective of the traditions of men and not the teachings of Christ. Such misapplication of the Scriptures can lead to false teachings. Christ placed such a high value on your life that He died so you might live. *He designed you with love, in His image. He knew you before you were in your mother's womb and He knit your bones together. You are fearfully and wonderfully made by the Great I AM. He designed you with a purpose and plan.* It is the evil one, *""The thief cometh not, but for to steal, and to kill, and to destroy: I am come that they might have life, and that they might have it more abundantly." John 10:10 KJV*

There is a progression to your disease, besetting sin, problem state that can be examined in the light of your life experiences. Fill in your "drug of choice," sin, disease, or dysfunction to examine the progression of your disease state in light of this five stage outline called "The Valley Chart," originally developed by Terrance Gorski. It's original use was for the treatment of alcoholism and drug addiction, later used in treating the family issues of co-dependency, family roles, enabling and the family system, used here to address all "besetting sin" in its modified format.

Follow the progression of the disease and or problem state and the reflection in the family. Where are you on the progression chart? One checked mark in a stage on the chart indicates progression to that stage. All characteristics do not need to be checked to indicate the disease has progressed to that stage.

**Exercise**

**PROGRESSION AND ONSET OF DISEASE REFLECT IN THE ENTIRE FAMILY:** *Circle the ones that apply to you and your family.*

*My family and I experience the following troubling situations:*

- ✓ Arguments

- ✓ Distrust

- ✓ Unhappiness

- ✓ Religious needs

- ✓ Denial (fantasy)

- ✓ Threats made-not carried out

- ✓ Blues

- ✓ Intolerance

- ✓ Suspicion

- ✓ Problems multiply

- ✓ Worry

- ✓ Irritability

*Without Help*

- ✓ Burdened by responsibility

- ✓ Loss of interest

- ✓ Imaginary illnesses

- ✓ Façade

- ✓ Uses prescription drugs

- ✓ Unnecessary surgeries and medical procedures in order to get more drugs

- ✓ Loss of self respect

- ✓ Remorse

- ✓ Social withdrawal

- ✓ Patent medicine use

- ✓ Indefinable fears

- ✓ Drug user

- ✓ Bankruptcy of alibis

- ✓ Jealousy

- ✓ Escape

- ✓ Blames others

- ✓ Isolation

- ✓ Infidelity

- ✓ Dishonesty

- ✓ Alibis

- ✓ Self neglect

- ✓ Irrational behavior

- ✓ Depression

- ✓ Self defense

- ✓ Extravagance

- ✓ Avoiding reference

- ✓ Seeks help

- ✓ Geographic cures: moving to a new city and/or running away from situations, people, places and things

***Bottom***

- ✓ Admits defeat

- ✓ Chronic depression

- ✓ Suicide attempts

***With Help***

- ✓ Hope

- ✓ Sincere desire for help

- ✓ Recognizes disease
- ✓ Acceptance
- ✓ Seeks help
- ✓ Recognition of role
- ✓ Need to control lessens
- ✓ Shares with other
- ✓ Becomes willing to change
- ✓ Cover-up ceases
- ✓ Begins to relax
- ✓ Developing optimism
- ✓ Daily living patterns change (rest, diet, sleep, hygiene)
- ✓ Diminishing fears
- ✓ Release
- ✓ Openness
- ✓ Trust
- ✓ Honesty

### *Recovery/Sanctification/Spiritual Examination*

- ✓ Return of self esteem
- ✓ Guilt is gone
- ✓ Peace of mind
- ✓ Makes amends
- ✓ New interests
- ✓ Confidence returns
- ✓ Happy
- ✓ Free
- ✓ Joyous
- ✓ Courage

✓ Love

✓ At ease with life

✓ Service

✓ New friends

✓ Appreciates spiritual values

✓ Respect of family and friends

✓ Enlightened with a higher level than possible before-bright future ahead.

(*See illustration "Onset of Disease Reflects in Family without Help")

**Exercise: Family System Application:** Using a different colored pen for each family member, circle each area that applies to each family member. Notice the level of progression in each member. Discuss your perceptions with each other. Notice how the whole system has been affected. Record your findings below:

| Family Member | Progression Level of Disease |
|---|---|
| Mom | _____ |
| Dad | _____ |
| Oldest Child | _____ |
| Middle Child | _____ |
| 2nd Middle Child | _____ |
| Youngest Child | _____ |

## Onset of Disease

- occasional use for relief
- preoccupation with (drug of choice)
- feelings of guilt
- memory lapses onset
- constant use of (drug of choice) bolstered with excuses
- tolerance increases (it takes more and more of the drug to get the same effects

## Crucial Phase Progression

- serial use of (drug of choice)
- increasing dependence on (drug of choice)
- unable to discuss problems
- efforts to control fail
- decrease in ability to stop when others do
- grandiose and aggressive behavior
- persistent remorse
- promises and resolutions fail
- family and friends avoided
- blackouts onset
- loss of other interest
- work and money troubles
- tickets/accidents

## Chronic Phase Progression

- tries geographic escapes
- tremors/withdrawal symptoms
- decrease in tolerance (no longer know what the "drug of choice" will do...the drug now has control)
- onset of lengthy intoxication or use
- moral deterioration
- impaired thinking
- using with inferiors
- indefinable fears
- unable to initiate action
- obsession with "drug of choice"
- unreasonable resentments
- vague spiritual desires
- physical deterioration/neglect of food
- legal problems/all alibis exhausted/complete defeat admitted
- hits bottom recovery or jails, institutions, death/suicide

copyright 2013 Dr. Phyllis Ericson-Davis and Rev. Carrol Davis

# DISEASE IS PROGRESSIVE, CHRONIC, AND CRUCIAL

Notice how far your disease has progressed. Notice how far your loved ones' disease has progressed. One check mark in any stage indicates progression of the diseased state to that stage.

In evaluating the dysfunctional behavior of the dependent person, we have found the following modified form of the "Valley Chart" helpful. It allows people to have some control and input into the evaluation of their problem(s). Again, any characteristic in the category indicates progression of the problem state to that level.

**Exercise: Progression of Diseased State, Besetting Sin, Dependency, Illness, Addiction**

Substitute your drug of choice for alcohol i.e. pornography, gambling, sex addiction, drugs, prescription medication etc., see stage one for an extensive list. This should add clarity to the evaluation of your particular addiction, sin, disease, problem state, co-dependency and the progression of your disease or problem. Circle each behavior that applies to you. In a different colored pen for each family member, circle each behavior that applies to that family member. What did you find out?

**\*PROGRESSION OF ADDICTIONS and DISEASE STATE**

- ✓ Occasional use for relief

- ✓ Having fun, partying

- ✓ Use to celebrate: happy occasions

- ✓ Use when depressed, sad, bad news, got a ticket, mad at you, fight with boss

- ✓ Use for ritual occasions e.g. work, business, toasts, weddings, etc.

- ✓ Preoccupation with _____ (DRUG OF CHOICE: Refer to chart)

- ✓ Feelings of guilt

- ✓ Memory lapses onset

- ✓ Constant use of _____ (DRUG OF CHOICE) for relief

- ✓ Use bolstered with excuses

- ✓ Tolerance increases (it takes more and more of the (DRUG OF CHOICE) to get the same effect)


**CRUCIAL PHASE**

- ✓ Serial use _____ (DRUG OF CHOICE). Consistent use. Rarely not using

- ✓ Increasing dependence _____ (DRUG OF CHOICE)

- ✓ Unable to discuss problems

- ✓ Efforts to control usage or actions fail

- ✓ Decrease in ability to stop when others do

- ✓ Grandiose and aggressive behavior

- ✓ Persistent remorse

- ✓ Promises and resolutions fail

- ✓ Family and friends avoided

- ✓ Blackouts onset

- ✓ Loss of other interests

- ✓ Work and money troubles

## CHRONIC PHRASE

- ✓ Tries geographic escapes (no permanent address, change location(s) frequently to avoid people, places, things, negative situations)

- ✓ Tremors/shaking/withdrawal symptoms

- ✓ Decrease in tolerance (no longer know what the "drug of choice" will do; it takes more and more of the "drug of choice" to get the same results).

- ✓ Onset of lengthy intoxication or use of the "drug of choice" (using for longer periods of time at a heavier level than before)

- ✓ Moral deterioration (doing things you never would have done before)

- ✓ Impaired thinking

- ✓ Using "drug of choice" with inferiors (using with criminals, dangerous person(s), unhealthy and unclean people, diseased people, people with poor hygiene)

- ✓ Indefinable fears

- ✓ Unable to initiate action (complete lack of motivation to change situation)

- ✓ Obsession with "drug of choice"

- ✓ Unreasonable resentments

- ✓ Vague spiritual desires

- ✓ Legal problems (divorce, separation, DUI, jail, prison, speeding tickets, domestic violence, conduct disorder, trouble with the law)

## BOTTOM

- ✓ All alibis exhausted (no longer makes excuses or tries to hide use/acting-out)

- ✓ Complete defeat admitted

- ✓ Neglect of food

- ✓ Physical deterioration

- ✓ Jails

- ✓ Institutions

✓ Suicide

✓ Death

✓ Tickets/accidents

(*See illustration Progression Crucial and Chronic)

Workshop participants break out into your groups and discuss your findings with each other. Give each other ten minutes to discuss your findings. Appoint a time keeper so that you stay on track and each person gets a turn. Appoint a representative from the group to share your findings with the large group.

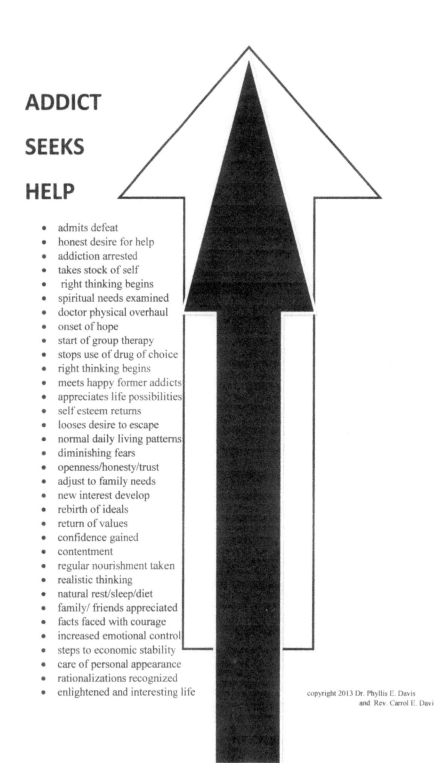

**ADDICT**

**SEEKS**

**HELP**

- admits defeat
- honest desire for help
- addiction arrested
- takes stock of self
- right thinking begins
- spiritual needs examined
- doctor physical overhaul
- onset of hope
- start of group therapy
- stops use of drug of choice
- right thinking begins
- meets happy former addicts
- appreciates life possibilities
- self esteem returns
- looses desire to escape
- normal daily living patterns
- diminishing fears
- openness/honesty/trust
- adjust to family needs
- new interest develop
- rebirth of ideals
- return of values
- confidence gained
- contentment
- regular nourishment taken
- realistic thinking
- natural rest/sleep/diet
- family/ friends appreciated
- facts faced with courage
- increased emotional control
- steps to economic stability
- care of personal appearance
- rationalizations recognized
- enlightened and interesting life

# *There is Hope: Righteousness is Passed Down to a Thousand Generations*

**R**EHABILITATION: Minimum 30 day inpatient treatment including individual, family and group therapy. Treatment programs with outpatient follow-up. 12 step programs: Al anon (those that love or are in relationship with an alcoholic), Nar Anon(those that love or are in a relationship with a drug addict), Co Da (Codependents), ACOA (adult children of alcoholics), AA (alcoholism), NA (drug addiction), SA(sex addicts, love addicts), COSA (those that are in love with or relationship with sex addict), GA (gamblers), OA (those with eating disorders), CR (Celebrate Recovery a Christ based 12 step program to deal with hurts, hang-ups and habits). If the group you need is not listed, call one of the above groups and they will be happy to direct you to a group near you. If you need in-patient treatment these groups can help you find appropriate treatment. Choose psychologists, social workers, biblical counselors and substance abuse counselors that specialize in dual diagnosis, family systems, and trauma issues. Medical doctors, psychiatrists, and some pastors, biblical counselors, psychologists, and social workers are not appropriate for your needs if they do not have the education, training, or specialized treatment intervention methods mentioned. They need additional training, education in family systems work and abuse issues; otherwise, they can do more harm than good.

**Exercise: Sanctification Results in a Shift in Attitudes and Behaviors**

As you move forward in the *sanctification* process the attitudes change as well. Circle the following character traits that apply to you. In a different colored pen for each family member in the sanctification process, circle all the character traits that apply to each member. What did you find out?

**God created you as a unique individual with plans for hope and a future**

✓ Honest desire for help

✓ Learns co-dependency is an illness

✓ Told addiction can be arrested

✓ Stops using "drug of choice"

✓ Meets normal, happy former addicts

✓ Takes stock of self

✓ Right thinking begins

✓ Spiritual needs examined

✓ Physical overhaul by doctor

✓ Onset of hope

✓ Start of group therapy

## RECOVERY

✓ Appreciation of life's possibilities

✓ Desires to follow the heart of Christ

✓ Diminishing fear of the unknown

✓ Self esteem returns

✓ Loses desire to escape

✓ Adjustment to family needs

✓ New interests develop

✓ Rebirth of ideals, understanding your mission, purpose,

✓ Confidence gained

✓ Appreciation of real values

✓ Contentment

✓ Group therapy continues

✓ Regular nourishment taken

✓ Realistic thinking

✓ Natural rest and sleep

✓ Family and friends appreciate effort

✓ New circle of stable friends

✓ Facts faced with courage

✓ Increased emotional control

✓ First steps to economic stability

✓ Care of personal appearance

✓ Rationalizations recognized

✓ Enlightened and interesting way of life opens

✓ Road ahead to higher levels than before.

(* See illustration Addict Seeks Help)

## Progression of Disease

- preoccupation with using
- increased tolerance
- gulps drinks or drugs
- morning use to get going
- change in eating habits
- change in sleeping patterns
- lack of motivation
- inability to concentrate
- change in grades at school or performance at work
- isolation from family and friends
- lack of interest in normal activities and hobbies

## Social Progression

- change in friends
- change or deterioration in places frequented
- time missed from school or work
- dropped performance at school or work
- decreased interest in hobbies and activities
- lying
- distorted thinking/inability to concentrate
- isolation from family

## Biological Progression

- use as a medicine
- blackouts (amnesia)
- brown outs (lapses in memory)
- morning tremors, or butterflies
- change in eating habits
- change in sleeping patterns
- weight loss, weight gain, loss of color, circles under eyes, trance, bulbous nose, red eyes , dilated or constricted pupils

- copyright 2013 Dr. Phyllis and Rev. Carrol  Davis

# "PROGRESSION OF DISEASE...
# SOCIAL... BIOLOGICAL"

We have found the modified "Valley Chart" helpful in assisting individuals to break through the denial and delusion of the problems in life. *We ask them to try to identify which level they are on in the process and or progression of their disease or problem state.* We tell them that if they have any of the checked aspects in the level, the disease has progressed to that level. In other words, all aspects of the level do not have to be present to diagnose that level of progression. All that is necessary is one checked characteristic of the progression to indicate the disease has reached that level.

### The Sins of the Father Pass on to the Second, Third and Fourth Generation

When dealing with addiction, disease, some problems, some hurts, hang-ups, habits, and besetting sin(s), you are dealing with biological, psychological, sociological, spiritual, and inherited factors that influence the disease and its progression.

*Biological* means that the actual body cells adapt to the "drug/action" to function. Abrupt termination of the "drug/action" produces withdrawal symptoms: (sweats, chills, fever, hallucinations, and shakes and in extreme cases without medical supervision, extreme illness and even death).

*Psychological* means that the person thinks they need the "drug/action" to function. Lack of the "drug/action" produces uncomfortable feelings. Use/action continues in spite of the negative consequences incurred. Use/action is "no fun," restlessness, irritability and anxiety occurs.

*Sociological* means that the "drug/action" is a part of an affiliation. It is a rite of passage. It is a part of belonging to a family system, fraternity, sorority, club, neighborhood, gang, society, or peer group. Use/action continues in spite of the negative consequences. This one will say, "All my friends do." "My family does." "What else is there to do?" Occasions revolve around use/behavior.

*Spiritual* means that the "drug/action" is used as a part of a religious ceremony, or part of the program and belief of the particular individual. Some use or act out the "drug of choice" contrary to their religious affiliation(s).

*Hereditary* means that the genes predisposing one to later need the "drug/action," are present in the brain of a baby that has never had a drink, used a drug, or acted out. Brain mapping is a technique used by scientist to discover the ability of the disease to be handed down from one generation to the next. It can however, skip a generation.

Once you have identified the problem state, the next stage in the process is identifying your defenses: the things that you do to keep the problem hidden from yourself, the things that you do to keep thinking that everything is alright you don't have a problem, even though your life testifies to the contrary. The "sins of the father" can go as many as six generations back, *"the third and fourth generations."* If one parent has a particular addiction, your chances of having that same addiction are fifty percent. If both parents had the particular addiction your chances double of having the same addiction. When the grandparents also had the particular addiction your chances of having the same problem, acting-out behavior, addiction, or besetting sin increases exponentially.

## Prayer

*Heavenly Father, I come before your throne of grace and ask that you review my life with me, bind up the spirits of denial and delusion in the name of your Son Jesus. Give me your wisdom as you search my heart, mind and spirit to remember the cost of my disease. Let me not leave anything out. Give me the honesty and integrity that your Son died to give me as I look over the events of the last several years, months and days. Bring to my mind persons, places and things that need to be included in my list and the cost of the disease. I ask for your grace and forgiveness for all of these things that are not pleasing to you. Bind up the enemy spirits of shame, confusion, denial, and delusion and let me remember and give an account honestly, confessing my sins to another so that I might heal according to your word.*

*It is in Jesus name I pray,*

*Amen*

## Exercise #1

An exercise that we have found helpful to break through the denial and delusion of the "drug/action" of choice, addiction, besetting sin, or problem state is to have the person calculate the cost to them in dollars and cents, relationships, education, work, and lost opportunities. The total usually amounts to thousands and thousands of dollars. Calculate the monetary loss of home, possessions, and the items hocked to support your habit as well as the cost of your "drug /action" of choice. What about the many lost educational opportunities, lost occupational and career choices, loss of health, loss of friends and family members, loss of time, loss of holidays spent with loved ones, spiritual loss and loss of relationship to God as well as lost values. Use the space below to calculate your losses.

Drug of Choice                                          Cost in Dollars and Cents

_____                              _____

_____                              _____

_____                              _____

_____                              _____

_____                              _____

Behavior Resulting From Use                                    Cost in Dollars and Cents

_____                    _____

_____                    _____

_____                    _____

Items Sold, Lost, or Pawned to Support, or                     Cost in Dollars and Cents

As a Result of Your Habit, Addiction, Use

_____                    _____

_____                    _____

_____                    _____

Time Lost From Work /School, Missed Jobs, Opportunities        Cost in Dollars and Cents

Promotions, Education, Being Fired, Inability to Function

_____                    _____

_____                    _____

_____                    _____

_____                    _____

Physical, Mental, Emotional Disease as a Result of Use         Cost in Dollars and Cents

_____                    _____

_____                    _____

_____                    _____

_____                    _____

_____                    _____

Destruction of Property As a Result of Use                    Cost in Dollars and Cents

_____                    _____

_____                    _____

_____                    _____

_____                    _____

Legal Issues, Fines, Bonds, Attorney's Fees, Divorce          Cost in Dollars and Cents

_____                    _____

_____                    _____

_____                    _____

_____                    _____

Loss of Family, Friends, Children, Affiliations, Things that

The Loss is Much More Than Dollars and Cents          Cost in Dollars and Cents Total $\_\_\_\_\_

_____

_____

_____

What did you discover? What do you think and how do you feel about your discoveries?

_____

_____

_____

Workshop Participants, take five minutes each to discuss what you discovered. What surprised you?

**Prayer**

*Heavenly Father, Holy Spirit, I thank you for your presence in my life. I thank you for going on this journey with me. Father, I ask that you send your angels ahead to prepare the way. Give me wisdom and discernment to ask the right questions. Give me ears to hear what you want me to hear. I pray Father, that you would cause people to tell me honestly anything that might be helpful to my sanctification process and the healing that you have gifted me with. Help me to say only what you would have me to say, think only what you would have me to think.*

*Give me a spirit of calm and the peace that passeth all understanding regardless of what I hear. Sit with me and give me your peace, I pray. I give you all the honor and glory. In Jesus name I pray, and by His stripes I am healed.*

*Amen*

**Exercise #2**

Meet with members of your family that knew or have knowledge of the first, second, third, and or fourth generation. Ask them questions to get a history of the "drug of choice," acting out behavior, addictions, problems, and besetting sin(s) in your family. You will start to see a pattern in the issues that trouble you. It may surprise you to see the "intergenerational" issues where you thought none existed.

Write down what you learned in your journal to share in group and with your partner.

_____

_____

_____

_____

_____

_____

_____

_____

_____

_____

_____

_____

_____

What did you find out? Did you discover any intergenerational sins, addictions, hurt, habits, hang-ups? What did you find out about mental disorders? What about legal problems, jail time, arrest? What did you find out about death, long term illnesses, and loss of family members due to abortion or adoption? Share your findings with your accountability person and/or your group.

_____

_____

_____

_____

_____

_____

_____

_____

_____

What defenses did your family members use when asked uncomfortable questions? The defenses your family uses to avoid pain and discomfort are probably some of the same defenses you have learned to use. Were they honest and authentic? Did they change the subject and avoid answering your questions? Are there family secrets that you were surprised to learn? Share with your accountability partner and your group what you learned.

_____

_____

_____

_____

_____

_____

_____

_____

_____

_____

_____

_____

_____

_____

_____

_____

_____

_____

_____

_____

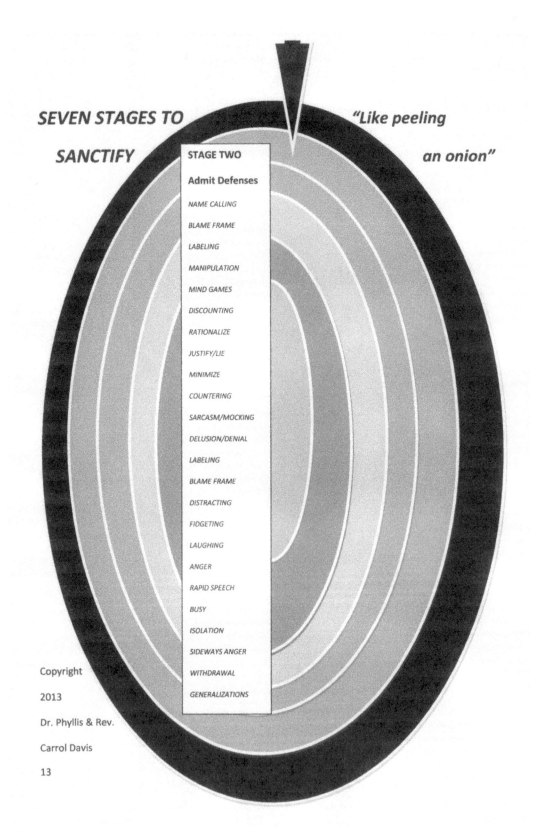

SEVEN STAGES TO
SANCTIFY

"Like peeling
an onion"

STAGE TWO

Admit Defenses

NAME CALLING

BLAME FRAME

LABELING

MANIPULATION

MIND GAMES

DISCOUNTING

RATIONALIZE

JUSTIFY/LIE

MINIMIZE

COUNTERING

SARCASM/MOCKING

DELUSION/DENIAL

LABELING

BLAME FRAME

DISTRACTING

FIDGETING

LAUGHING

ANGER

RAPID SPEECH

BUSY

ISOLATION

SIDEWAYS ANGER

WITHDRAWAL

GENERALIZATIONS

# Section 2:

## *The Masks You Wear*

# STAGE TWO DEFENSES: RECOGNIZING THE OUTWARD SIGNS

*"The truth shall set you free." John 8:32 KJV*

*A* *Admit Defenses Used To Cover Pain*

*I admit that I use defenses to keep you from knowing how I really feel and to cover my pain. I am not completely honest and authentic about my feelings.*

You all have certain things you do to avoid uncomfortable feelings. You all present one image to the public while having that private image that only your closest friends and associates know about. It is your ability to be "at choice" about using your mask(s) or defense(s) that help you to make healthy choices and decisions. There is the mask that your friends at work and school know, another that those at Sunday school recognize. There is the mask of the "mom" or "dad" and the mask of the "little child." All of these different "masks" represent different parts of your personality or persona. Some people know only the teacher or the student. More intimate friends know all aspects of your personalities.

## *Boundaries*

Stated another way, you all need to have boundaries. Jesus did. He had a certain circle of friends that He shared the most intimate issues of his life with (James and John). He had circles of thousands that He met in passing while delivering the "Sermon on the Mount" and at the waters of baptism with John the Baptist. Jesus shared his closest, most intimate issues with his closest disciples. All people did not know Him in the same way.

Boundaries can be in regard to your physical bodies, your intellectual self, and your emotional self, your sexual and spiritual self. Different people and their different levels of intimacy with you determine with whom you share these different aspects of your person. Some people are not "safe" people. It is not healthy to share truly intimate details with such unsafe persons. Cloud and Townsend wrote a fantastic book on the subject of "Safe People," recommended reading for anyone who lacks appropriate boundaries to be used as a tool to help rebuild what was lost. To repeat the words of their work or to try to improve on the subject would do the topic an injustice. The subject of boundaries is mentioned here to make one aware of areas of brokenness and areas where healing is needed.

The area of abuse will point to the area where boundaries need to be rebuilt. For example, if one was sexually abused, the problem area(s) of their lives will most probably be sexual in nature. Sexual boundaries will need to be rebuilt: what is appropriate touching, by whom, in what situations, as well as what is not.

If one was beaten as a child, the adult will need to rebuild physical boundaries. They will not know what normal is and may touch people without permission, hug others inappropriately, or lack skills of discipline with their own children.

When children are emotionally abused, they may be unable to access their entire God given emotions. They may cry when they are angry instead of expressing their irritation in a given situation. This is common in females who have been emotionally abused. Males tend to express anger and are unable to get in touch with their sadness. The adult has to rebuild these broken boundaries.

Intellectual abuse will result in the now adult/child's inability to express themselves in an effective way, stammering or stuttering, absent mindedness, or confusion. Many times the intellectual abuse is combined with emotional abuse as the child was growing up to statements such as "You are just stupid."....."You don't know how to do anything." ..."You mess up everything you touch." ....."Just don't try."..."You'll just get it wrong."

*Sanctification* rebukes these lies of Satan and replaces the lies with the truth of God, The Bible:

*"You are fearfully and wonderfully made."...."You can do all things through Christ who strengthens you."....."Nothing is impossible with God".......".Commit all your plans to Him and you will succeed."*

In this stage of the process you are focused on the question: "Exactly what are your defenses?" You want to be able to drop the façade, the masks that you wear, and focus on feelings: the thoughts and feelings behind the masks.

Below is a partial list of these behaviors and the biblical comparatives. Again if you are not certain as to which of these defenses are yours, ask God. He knows. Ask Him to lead you to the persons that will be honest in helping you discover what your defenses are. Ask your accountability person, your group, or in some cases, your family what they think your defenses are. You can use prayer and the "rule of three" to help you.

**Prayer**

*Heavenly Father, I come before your throne of grace, thanking you for my salvation and the gift of sanctification that your son died to give me. Father I ask that the Holy Spirit search my heart and mind and bring to my remembrance the ways I have avoided uncomfortable feelings. Bring to my mind the defenses I have used to cover my pain so that I can admit my character defects. Help me submit to you any ways that do not line up with your word for sanctification. In Jesus name and by His power I pray. Amen*

**STAGE TWO: DEFENSES**

*Matthew 12:36 and 37 AMP (Overview of Defenses and the Biblical Comparisons)*
*36"But I tell you, on the Day of Judgment, men will have to give account for every idle (inoperative, non-working) word they speak. 37 For by your words you will be justified and acquitted, and by your words you will be condemned and sentenced."*

1. **DENIAL: Refusing to accept and acknowledge the truth of a matter**

*1 John 1: 8, 9 KJV*
*"If we say that we have no sin, we deceive ourselves, and the truth is not in us, 9 if we confess our sins, He is faithful and just to forgive us our sins, and to cleanse us from all unrighteousness."*

2. **RAPID SPEECH: Talking incessantly without clearly communicating a particular thought or idea**

*James 1:19 KJV*
*"Wherefore, my beloved brethren, let every man be swift to hear, **slow to speak**, slow to wrath."*

3. **ANGER: Loud, course speech, and gesturing, sometimes vulgar language, usually driven by fear**

*James 1:19 AMP*
*"Understand this, my beloved brethren, let every man be quick to hear (a ready listener), slow to speak, slow to take offense and to get angry."*

*Ephesians 4:26, 27 AMP*

*"When angry, do not sin: do not ever let your wrath (your exasperation, your fury or indignation) last until the sun goes down. 27 Leave no (such) room or foothold for the devil (give no opportunity to him)."*

4. **FIDGETTING: Constant body movement, pacing, folding papers, playing with objects while speaking**

*Philippians 4: 8, 9 KJV*

*"Finally, brethren, whatsoever things are true, whatsoever things are honest, whatsoever things are just, whatsoever things are pure, whatsoever things are lovely, whatsoever things are of good report; if there be any virtue, and if there be any praise, think on these things. Those things, which ye have both learned, and received, and heard, and seen in me, do: and the God of peace shall be with you." Paul, speaking to the Philippians*

5. **LAUGHING: Inappropriate laughing to cover ones true feelings**

*Ephesians 5: 4 KJV*

*"...Neither filthiness, nor foolish talking, nor jesting, which are not convenient: (improper) but rather giving of thanks. "*

6. **SIDE WAYS ANGER: Directing anger at a less threatening target than the person one is really angry with. ...snide remarks**

*Ephesians 4:26, 27 AMP*

*"When angry, do not sin; do not ever let your wrath (your exasperation, your fury or indignation) last until the sun goes down. Leave no (such) room or foothold for the devil (give no opportunity to him)."*

7. **BUSY: Moving about, pacing, nail biting etc.**

*Luke 10:39-42 KJV (The Story of Mary and Martha)*

*39... "Mary sat at Jesus feet and heard His words "*

*40"Martha was cumbered about much serving, and came to him (Jesus)"*

*41"Jesus answered...Martha thou art careful and troubled about many things:"*

*42"But one thing is needful: and Mary hath chosen that good part which shall not be taken away from her."*

8. **ISOLATION/WITHDRAWING: Sitting in the corner alone while in a group, staying by oneself, refusing to speak ones mind**

*Hebrews 10:25 KJV*

*"Not forsaking the assembling of ourselves together, as the manner of some is; but exhorting one another; and so much the more, as you see the day approaching."*

*Hebrews 10:25 AMP*

*"Not forsaking or neglecting to assemble together (as believers), as is the habit of some people, but admonishing (warning, urging, encouraging) one another, and all the more faithfully as you see the day approaching."*

9. **DELUSION: Believing a fantasy, falsehood, deceiving oneself**

*John 8:32 KJV*

*"You shall know the truth and the truth shall make you free." (It is a Process: "shall make")*

(truth: the Son of God; Truth, the word of God; truth, the power to set you free; Truth, the Son of God; Truth, the commands and teachings of Christ; truth) See verses 31 through 47

*2 Corinthians 10:5*

*"Casting down imaginations, and every high thing that exalteth itself against the knowledge of God, and bringing into captivity every thought to the obedience of Christ."*

## 10. DISTRACTING: Changing the subject or the focus of the conversation

*Matthew 5:37 AMP*

*"Let what you say be simple 'Yes' or 'No'; anything more than this comes from evil."*

*(Be a person of your word.....Be accountable)*

## 11. BLAME FRAME: Refusing to be held accountable for one's failures while placing the accountability on someone else

*Genesis 3:12, 13 KJV (The story of Adam, Eve and the Serpent blaming each other)*

*"And the man said, the woman whom thou gravest to be with me, she gave me of the tree, and I did eat. 13 and the Lord God said unto the woman, what is this that thou hast done? And the woman said, the serpent beguiled me, and I did eat."*

## 12. LABELING/GENERALIZATIONS: Judging hearts and motives, only God can do, such as:

All, Never, Have To, Must, Only, Always. Examples: They never say the right thing. *Counter with:* Never...Not even once? He is always late. *Counter with:* Always... Not on time even once?

*Matthew 7:1, 2 KJV*

*"Judge not, that ye be not judged. 2 For with what judgment ye judge, ye shall be judged; and with what measure ye mete, it shall be measured to you again."*

13. **NAME CALLING: Foul language, calling people their failures…not separating the person from the behavior**

*Proverbs 18:21 KJV*

*"Death and Life are in the power of the tongue: and they that love it shall eat the fruit thereof." Matthew 5:22 KJV*

*"But I say unto you, that whosoever is angry with his brother without a cause shall be in danger of the judgment: and whosoever shall say to his brother, Raca shall be in danger of the council: but whosoever shall say Thou fool, shall be in danger of hell fire."*

14. **MIND GAMES: Turning the focus of accountability on the person asking the questions…like a lawyer. (Luke10:25-29)**

*Philippians 2:5 KJV*

*"Let the mind be in you, which was also in Christ Jesus."*

15. **RATIONALIZATION / JUSTIFICATION: Making excuses for ones behavior instead of being accountable… e.g. I would not have gone drinking if you had not made me angry.**

*Exodus 23:7 KJV*

*"Keep thee far from a false matter; and the innocent and righteous slay thou not; for I will not justify (defend) the wicked."*

*Luke 10:25-29 (The story of Jesus, the lawyer, and eternal life…the lawyer tries to defend his failures because he knows he can not or has not kept the law …the law of love)*
*29'But he (the lawyer), willing to justify himself, said unto Jesus, and who is my neighbor?"*

16. **LIES: Not speaking the truth, living a hypocritical life.....saying one thing and doing something else**

*1 John 1:6 KJV*

*"If we say that we have fellowship with him, and walk in darkness, we lie, and do not the truth."*

*John 8:44 KJV*

*"Ye are of your father, the devil, and the lust of your father ye will do. He was a murderer from the beginning, and abode not in the truth, because there is no truth in him. When he speaketh a lie, he speaketh of his own; for he is a liar and the father of it. "*

17. **DISCOUNTING: Ignoring one's presence, thoughts, ideas, feelings, abilities, accomplishments, achievements, devaluing a person's worth.**

*Romans 12:3 AMP*

*For by the grace (unmerited favor of God) given to me, I warn everyone among you not to estimate and think of himself more highly than he ought (not to have an exaggerated opinion of his own importance), but to rate his ability with sober judgment, each according to the degree of faith appointed by God to him."*

18. **MINIMIZING: Making light of something; giving it less weight or importance than is realistic**

*Ephesians 2:10 KJV*

*"For we are His workmanship, created in Christ Jesus unto good works, which God hath before ordained that we should walk in them."*

*Romans 8:29 KJV*

*"For whom he did foreknow, he also did predestinate to be conformed to the image of his Son, that he might be the firstborn among many brethren."*

*Isaiah 44:24 KJV*

"Thus saith the Lord, thy redeemer, and he that formed thee from the womb, I am the Lord that maketh all things; that stretched forth the heavens alone; that spreadeth abroad the earth by myself."

*Psalms 139:13, 14 AMP*

"For you did form my inward parts. You did knit me together in my mother's womb. I will confess and praise you for you are fearful and wonderful and for the awful wonder of my birth! Wonderful are your works, and that my inner self knows right well."

19. **COUNTERING / ARGUING: I say it's white, you say it is black. No matter what the topic of discussion, I know more about it than anyone else. I have a need to be right. My opinion is the correct one.**

*James 4:1, 2 KJV*

"From whence come wars and fightings among you? Come they not hence, even of your lusts that war in your members? Ye lust, and have not; ye kill and desire to have and cannot obtain: ye fight and war, yet ye have not, because ye ask not. "

*Job 7:25 KJV*

"How forcible are right words! But what doth your arguing reprove?"

*1 Corinthians 3:2, 3 KJV*

2 "I have fed you with milk, and not with meat: for hitherto ye were not able to bear it, neither yet now are ye able. 3 For ye are yet carnal: for whereas there is among you envying, and strife, and divisions, are ye not carnal, and walk as men?"

**20. SARCASM / MOCKING: Sarcasm is sideways anger. Righteous anger is directed at the problem in a direct way or used to set boundaries, and/or change circumstances.**

*Genesis 4:9*

*"Am I my brother's keeper?"*

*Matthew 27:29*

*"...Hail, King of the Jews!"*

**21. MANIPULATION: Shrewd management and control by artful means; controlling.**

*2 Corinthians 4:2*

*"But have renounced the hidden things of dishonesty, not walking in craftiness, nor handling the word of God deceitfully...."*

©Rev. Carrol and Dr. Phyllis Davis copyright 2013, revised 2014 (Defenses and Biblical Comparison)

**Prayer:**

*Heavenly Father, Holy Spirit I ask you to be present with me today as I work to let down my guard and defenses in order to submit the broken areas of my life to you for healing.*

*Father, I bind up the spirits of confusion, distraction, delusion and denial that wish to stop, block, and or interfere in anyway with the healing that the true Lord Jesus has for me today.*

*I pray Father that you would give me wisdom and discernment according to your word that tells me when I ask you will give to me liberally.*

*I thank you Father for your Son who died on the cross for the forgiveness of my sins and I claim the healing that the stripes on his back bore for me, "By His stripes we are healed."*

*Thank you for all you have done in my life and the lives of others. Thank you for all you are going to do. It is in gratitude to you for your provision and in the name of your Son Jesus that I pray.*
*Amen*

**Exercise:**

Think of a number between one and four. If your number is one, go to corner one. If your number is two, go to corner two. If your number is three, go to corner three. If your number is four go to corner four. If you could not think of a number, or if you thought of a number other than one through four, go to the center of the room.

Break up into groups of five. Using the above list try to identify what defenses you use to cover your pain and tell the group about the defenses you use. Go around the circle until every group member has had a turn.

If you are unable to identify the defenses you use to cover your pain, go back to the list you made in stage one. Tell the group about your addictions, life experiences/problems, hurts, hang-ups and habits; sin and disobedience to God's word, physical disease, psychiatric disorder, etc. from the categories in stage one. As an alternative, you may choose to tell of an embarrassing story in lieu of the stage one categories you have identified. After you finished your disclosure, go around the circle and let the group members tell you what they think your defenses are. Let each group member have a turn.

Once you have received feed back from the group as to what they think your defenses are, consider their response. Do you agree? Do you disagree? If you are still having problems identifying your defenses, raise your hand and let a leader know you need help.

If you still disagree with the feedback that you received, take your list of defenses home and ask your spouse, a close friend, boyfriend, girlfriend, prayer warrior, or sponsor what they think your defenses are.

We use what is termed the rule of three. If you get the same feedback from three separate sources that you know care about you and have nothing to lose or gain by the feedback they give, consider their responses valid and proceed. Pray and ask God to confirm or deny your feedback over the next couple of days and weeks. Proceed in the process as if the feedback you received is valid.

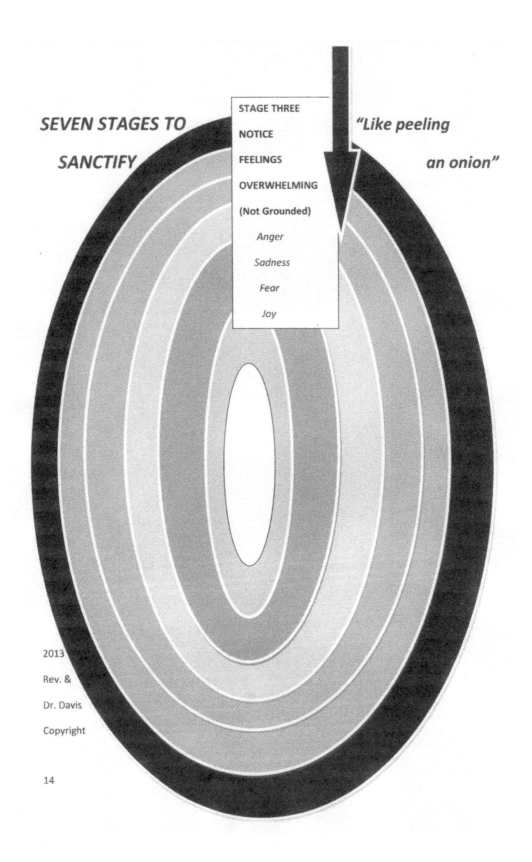

*SEVEN STAGES TO*

*SANCTIFY*

*"Like peeling*

*an onion"*

STAGE THREE

NOTICE

FEELINGS

OVERWHELMING

(Not Grounded)

*Anger*

*Sadness*

*Fear*

*Joy*

2013

Rev. &

Dr. Davis

Copyright

14

# Section 3:

## *Whenever the feeling is bigger than the event, it is always about your history.*

# STAGE THREE: OVERCOMING YOUR FEELINGS

*"Keep thy heart with all diligence for out of it are the issues of life."*

*Proverbs 4:23 KJV*

*"The heart is deceptive above all things, and desperately wicked: who can know it?"*

*Jeremiah 29:11 KJV*

*N* *Notice Overwhelming Feelings/Thoughts*

*I admit that my feelings and thoughts sometimes overwhelm me. My thoughts and feelings are not what they should be.*

If you allow your feelings to direct your paths, if you only do what you feel like doing, if you always say exactly what you think and feel, your life will fall apart at the seams. You are to recognize your feelings and understand exactly what you are thinking that is driving your feelings. The Apostle Paul says to take your thoughts captive to the obedience of Christ. In other words, if what you are thinking is not of God, you are to recognize the thought as negative and from the author of lies, Satan himself, and replace the thought with what God says about the particular subject. Using Scripture to defeat the lies of Satan is the example set for you by Christ in His wilderness experience. A life driven by the lies of Satan leads you to your own wilderness experience, not to the abundant life Christ has promised.

It is part of the sanctification process and growth in Christ to learn to take your thoughts captive. It takes practice. Many times people confuse what they feel with what they think. It takes practice to learn to separate thoughts from feelings. It can also take some practice to notice a feeling and attach a name to it. Many times people call a thought a feeling. In order to help with the process, you can narrow down the feelings that you have into just a few categories. Most feelings fall into different degrees of: ANGER, SADNESS, FEAR, and JOY. Until one is comfortable identifying feelings, it is best to start off with this short list of feelings. Get a trusted friend, pastor, teacher, dialogue partner, prayer partner to help you start.

## GROUNDED FEELINGS

Sometimes your feelings are grounded in reality. Meaning when you feel angry, you know exactly why you have that feeling, and you can tie the emotion to a particular event, person, interaction, or set of circumstances. *However, if the feeling is bigger than the event, it is probably about your history, your past.* An example might be: Someone accidentally cuts you off while driving down the road. They drive by waving an apology, and an "I'm sorry." One week later you are still angry, fuming, and can not stop talking about the situation. *The feeling is bigger than the event.* An event, person, place or thing in your history, or your past has been *"triggered* "by the current situation. Your "buttons" have been pushed. Your feelings are not grounded in reality.

## UNGROUNDED FEELINGS

Sometimes the feelings are ungrounded in reality. Meaning when you feel sad you have no idea why. To your knowledge nothing has happened to cause this emotion. There is no particular event, person, place, or thing tied to this negative emotion. This is what you call an ungrounded feeling. The Bible teaches in *Jeremiah 17:9* how your hearts deceive you, *"the heart is deceptive above all things, and desperately wicked: who can know it?"*

At the bottom of most problem states are these ungrounded feelings. You believe that if you are feeling sad that you need an explanation for your sadness. Sometimes this unexplained sadness can be traced back to the recorder in your head mimicking the words of a parent, "Keep that up and I'll give you something to cry about."

## BUTTONS and TRIGGERS

Have you ever heard the expression, "She just pushes my buttons?" What the person is probably expressing is that something about the person causes them to have uncomfortable feelings. Most likely those uncomfortable, un-grounded feelings are caused by something in the person's history that they are not even aware of. Many times when you are annoyed by someone else's behavior or actions, it is really your past issues reflected in them and their behavior that is annoying you. Check out your history before responding to outside stimuli. Keep your side of the street clean. In other words look inside your own issues to resolve problems first.

### *The Story of Beatrice*

An example of this would be from work with a particular patient, whom you will call Beatrice. Beatrice came to the office one day exclaiming how much she hated the smell of beans. She could not stand to smell them, eat them, or watch some one else eat them. She hated beans!!! This was somewhat curious as beans are an inanimate object that does not usually evoke such strong emotions in a person. We decided to explore this curious situation.

Beatrice was instructed to go back into her history to see when she first developed such a strong emotional reaction to "beans." We went back to a time when Beatrice was a child of about 4 years old. Like most four year old children, Beatrice was anxious to please her parents.

117

She decided one afternoon, when left alone, that she would cook the family's dinner. Too small to reach the stove on her own, she dragged the old wooden stool over to the stove and proceeded to climb to the top. Struggling, she dragged the big pot out of the cupboard, filled it with water, and put in the beans to cook. She turned on the stove. Proud of her accomplishments, she skipped off to play, forgetting the entire endeavor.

As she scooted the little cars through the dirt in the garden out back, a loud voice boomed from the kitchen door. "Uh Oh," it was her father and he was in a rage. Out he came yelling and screaming as he approached her. His huge hand swung down and scooped her up with one arm, dragging her to the house. "Stop that hurts," she yelled, to no avail.

"I'll teach you," He screamed.

"What did I do? What did I do?" the little girl thought to herself.

The Dad threw the little girl on the bed and gave her the trashing of her life. One she would never forget. Beatrice could smell the beans burning on the stove as her Dad struck her blow after blow.

This is similar to many recants of repressed memories that cause persons to have strong emotional reactions to things in the here and now. The "beans" were the trigger to remind Beatrice of the unpleasant encounter with her father. Because the memory of the event was repressed, Beatrice had no control over the surfacing of the unpleasant memories. Anytime she saw or smelled beans, the negative emotions were triggered and she had to re-live the negative emotions all over again.

Beatrice had to have her sadness, fear and anger over the events that happened to that little four year old child. She had to be reassured that it was not her fault. She had to be told that no little girl should be treated that way by her father. She had to remember all the ways this experience had affected her as an adult. She had to thoroughly process or work through the memory.

Then, and only then, she had to forgive her father. First, we imagined him sitting in a chair and then Beatrice visualized him sitting there. She talked about what he was wearing, the look on his face, the sound of his voice, and the way it made her feel. The father was instructed to be bound to the chair until Beatrice was finished telling him exactly what she thought and how she felt about what happened to her.

Next Beatrice told her father that she forgave him for hurting her, for the sound of his voice, for the look on his face, for the way he made her feel. She told him how his actions had affected her and how angry she had been with him. She told him how sad it was for her that he was not the kind of father that God created him to be. Next she told him she was just a little girl looking for her Daddy's approval. She told him she didn't need his approval any longer, that now she seeks only God's approval.

Then Beatrice told her father that she forgave him not because what he did was OK, because it was not. She forgave him because the Lord commanded her to. Then she released her father to her HEAVENLY FATHER'S perfect justice.

Next Beatrice asked God to forgive her for her un-forgiveness, for carrying this burden for so long, for failure to follow the word of God. She asked that He set her free and fill her with His healing energy. In the spaces where negativity resided, she asked Him to replace that energy with love, creativity and freedom in Jesus' name.

She next told the enemies of destruction to flee. They had no place in her life. She had forgiven her father and asked the Lord Jesus to forgive her. She then commanded the demons of un-forgiveness, sadness, fear and anger to leave. She asked Jesus to replace the negative emotions with healing energy.

God created you with all of your feelings. The problem is that you label your feelings as positive or negative, and if you don't keep them in check, you make bad decisions based on your feelings, which are not grounded in reality. A slogan in the "recovery" community that works well is: "Do the next right thing; your feelings will catch up."

When those feelings are nagging at you, and will not go away, no matter how many times you choose the right path, it might be time to explore their origin. You need to get to the core issue and resolve the situation, once and for all.

## THOUGHTS and FEELINGS

Examining your thoughts can take care of a lot of your negative feelings. It is what you think that determines how you feel. How you feel can determine how you act. If you change what you are thinking, you can improve your mood; change your feelings, and actions:

The Apostle Paul, a devout follower of Christ, expresses his dilemma. Obviously, a Christian, he still struggles: *"For I do not understand my own actions, (I am baffled, bewildered) I do not practice or accomplish what I wish, but I do the very thing that I loathe, (which my moral instincts condemn). Romans 7:15 AMP*

**Exercise: Thoughts and Feelings**

Read the two examples below. Underline the thoughts expressed in these scenarios, circle the feelings.

**Scenario #1:**

John's boss tells him, as he leaves the office one evening, that he needs to see him in his office at 9:00 the following morning. (The actual event)

John thinks that he is not as good as some of the other employees at his job. He sometimes feels stupid. (John's thoughts)

The closer John gets to home the worse he feels. When he arrives home he has a headache, he is angry, sad and full of fear. (John's feelings)

His wife meets him at the door and asks how his day went. John barks at her in a gruff voice, "It was horrible and I wish you would get out of my way." (John's actions)

**Scenario #2:**

Notice how a change in John's thoughts, change his feelings and his actions when the actual event stays the same:

John's boss tells him, as he leaves the office one evening, that he needs to see him in his office at 9:00 the following morning. (The actual event stays the same)

John thinks that he might get the raise he has been hoping for. (John's thoughts)

The closer John gets to home the more excited he feels. When he arrives home he has a happy spirit, is full of joy and expectation. (John's feelings)

His wife meets him at the door and asks how his day went. John hugs her tightly and says, "It was great. How was yours?" (John's actions)

The first scenario ended in a fight between John and his wife. The second scenario ended in a pleasant evening. The only difference(s) in the two scenarios are John's thoughts and feelings. When John has positive thoughts, his feelings are positive and his actions reflect the same. Negative thoughts caused John to have negative feelings, and his actions caused problems in his relationships.

The Scriptures have already taught you this principle, if you had only known how to rightly apply the word of God to your life problems, *"...whatsoever things are true, whatsoever things are honest, whatsoever things are just, whatsoever things are pure, whatsoever things are lovely, whatsoever things are of good report; if there be any virtue, and if there be any praise, think on these things." Philippians 4:8 KJV* *"Study to shew thyself approved unto God, a workman that needeth not to be ashamed, rightly dividing the word of truth." 2 Timothy 2:15*

John's negative actions could be changed at any point in the above illustration. If he changes what he thinks, if he changes what he feels, if he changes what he does, the resulting argument between John and his wife could have been avoided. The Scriptures refer to this principle*: "For as he thinketh in his heart, so is he." Proverbs 23:7a You are told to take your thoughts captive to the obedience of Christ. (2 Corinthians 10:5)*

What did you learn from the above exercise? Is there anything the wife could have thought or felt differently that might have changed the outcome? Share with your group. (Hint: What does the bible teach me about offenses? What do you know about boundaries? What do you know about detachment?) Record your thoughts below. Share with your sponsor, accountability partner or small group.

_____

_____

_____

_____

_____

_____

_____

_____

_____

_____

_____

Many times your negative thoughts are rooted in childhood. A parent, a teacher, an aunt, an uncle, a grandparent, a preacher, a coach, a neighbor, a friend, a Sunday school teacher programmed your child brain just like a computer. The now adult/child is running on the programs of the past. Many times these negative programs and thoughts are out of your conscious awareness. You are not even aware of the negative thoughts that promote the lies of Satan rather than the truth of God. You continue to tell yourself the negative statements, just as you heard them spoken to you in childhood. Sometimes these beliefs are referred to as "the parent tapes." These unconscious thoughts and beliefs must be examined in light of the truth of God's word. Negative tapes must be changed to reflect the truth.

When incidents of trauma happen to children they sometimes believe a lie based on what they think is happening, given a child's experiences and frame of reference. The incident that causes a child to feel abandoned, shame, fear, powerless, tainted, invalidated, hopeless or confused may not be abusive, but rather what the child believes to be happening. When the child has one of these experiences, there is usually an accompanying lie that goes with the repressed memory of the event. The lie needs to be processed and replaced with the truth of God's word.

Remember the slogan you all heard in school as one child taunts another, "Sticks and stones can break my bones, but words can never hurt me." This is a lie from the pit of hell. God's word says, *"Death and life are in the power of the tongue." Proverbs 18:21a*

**THOUGHTS**: It is your "negative" thoughts that cause "negative" feelings. Change your thoughts, change your feelings. *"As a man thinketh in his heart, so is he."* Proverbs 23:7

**Exercise:**

See the list below to identify some of the "negative" thoughts that may be causing you problems.

Some common lies that people have been programmed to believe and the biblical counterparts are as follows. Circle all the lies that you have believed and start daily affirmations of the truth from God's word. It takes many more positive messages to over come the negative ones. It takes a minimum of thirty one days to change a habit or belief. Spend the next thirty one days reprogramming your mind with the refreshing truth of God's word.

### LIES VS THE TRUTH FROM GOD'S WORD

- ✓ I don't matter. *I am God's child. John 1:12*

- ✓ I am not needed. *God has plans for my future. Jeremiah 29:11*

- ✓ I am not wanted. *I am adopted into God's Family. Ephesians 1:5*

- ✓ I am not cared for. *I am Christ's friend. John 15:15*

- ✓ I am guilty. *I have been justified... Romans 5:1*

- ✓ I am all alone. *I am united with the Lord. 1 Corinthians 6:17*

- ✓ I am worthless. *I am bought with a price; I belong to God. 1 Corinthians 6:19,* 20

- ✓ I don't belong. *I am a member of Christ's Body. 1 Corinthians 12:27*

- ✓ I am tainted. *I am His workmanship. Ephesians 2:10*

- ✓ I am unclean. *I am cleansed from all unrighteousness. 1 John 1:9*

- ✓ I am evil, perverted. *I am a saint. Ephesians 1:1*

- ✓ I am shameful. *I am the righteousness of God in Christ Jesus. 2 Corinthians 5:21*

- ✓ I am damaged. *I am fearfully and wonderfully made. Psalms 139:14*

✓  I am a mistake, broken. *He foreknew me in my mother's womb. Psalms 139:13*

✓  I am unwanted. *I have been adopted as God's child. Ephesians 1:5*

✓  No one cares. *I have access to God thru the Holy Spirit. Ephesians 2:18*

✓  My sins are too great. *I have been redeemed and forgiven. Colossians 1:14*

✓  I'm flawed. *I am complete in Christ. Colossians 2:10*

✓  I am condemned. *I am free forever from condemnation. Romans 8:1,2*

✓  I am a disaster. *I am assured all works together for good. Romans 8:28*

✓  It's my fault. *I am free from any charge against me. Romans 8:31-34*

✓  No one loves me. *I can not be separated from the love of God. Romans 8:35-39*

✓  I am damned. *I am established, anointed, sealed by God. 2 Corinthians 1:21, 22*

✓  They will harm me. *I am hidden with Christ in God. Colossians 3:3*

✓  I'm not worth it. *God bought me with a price. 1 Corinthians 6:20*

✓  There is no good thing for me. *I am confident that the good work God has begun in me will be perfected. Philippians 1:6*

✓  I have no value. *I am a citizen of heaven. Philippians 3:20*

✓  I am terrified. *I have not been given a spirit of fear, but of power, love and a sound mind. 2 Timothy 1:7*

✓  No one will help me. *I can find grace and mercy in time of need. Hebrews 4:16*

✓  I will be destroyed. *I am born of God; the evil one cannot touch me. 1 John 5:18*

✓  I have no value. *I am the salt and light of the earth. Matthew 5:13, 14*

✓  I am powerless. *I am a branch of the true vine, a channel of His life. John 15:1, 5*

✓  I am worthless. *I have been chosen and appointed to bear much fruit. John 15:16*

✓  I have no value. *I am a personal witness of Christ's. Acts 1: 8*

✓  I don't matter. *I am God's temple. 1 Corinthians 3:16*

✓  I am not needed. *I am a minister of reconciliation for God. 2 Corinthians 5:17-21*

✓  I'm worthless. *I am God's co-worker. 2 Corinthians 6:1, 1 Corinthians 3:9*

✓  I don't belong. *I am seated with Christ in the heavenly realm. Ephesians 2:6*

- ✓ I'm dirty. *I am God's workmanship. Ephesians 2:10*

- ✓ I'm bound. *I may approach God with freedom and confidence. Ephesians 3:12*

- ✓ I can't. *I can do all things thru Christ who strengthens me. Philippians 4:13*

- ✓ I am doomed. *I am sealed with the Holy Spirit, my guarantee. Ephesians 4:30*

- ✓ I have no way out. *I can do all things through Christ who strengthens me. Philippians 4:13*

- ✓ I am powerless. *I am a child of God. John 1:12*

- ✓ I am hopeless. *He makes all things new. 2 Corinthians 5:17*

- ✓ I am helpless. *The power of God lives in me. Acts 1: 8*

- ✓ I am poor. *God shall supply all my needs according to His riches in glory in Christ Jesus. Philippians 4:19*

- ✓ I am overwhelmed. *He that is in me is greater than he who is in the world. 1 John 4:4*

- ✓ I don't know what to do. *Christ became wisdom to me from God. 1 Corinthians 1:30*

- ✓ I can not figure this out. *God gives wisdom generously when I ask Him. James 1:5*

- ✓ I am afraid, worried. *I cast all my cares on Christ who cares for me. 1 Peter 5:7*

- ✓ I am defeated. *God always leads me in triumph. 2 Corinthians 2:14*

- ✓ Everyone is against me. *If God is for me who can be against me? Romans 8:31*

- ✓ I am cursed. *Christ redeemed me from the curse of the law. Galatians 3:13, 14*

- ✓ I am in bondage. *Where the Spirit of the Lord is there is liberty. 2 Corinthians 3:17*

- ✓ I can not handle it. *I take courage knowing that Jesus overcame the world and its tribulations. John 16:33*


As you read the above list, notice which truths do not seem to fit. Which ones do you find hard to believe? Remember to separate who you are from what you have done. God hates the sin (behavior); God loves the sinner (person). God turns His back on sin; the sinner He never leaves or forsakes, is with you always, even to the end of the age. Focus on God's word that addresses that particular false belief that you have internalized. Post the word of God, the Truth, on post- it notes in different colors throughout your house. Say the word of God out loud to yourself. Play music with lyrics that sing the truth of God.

Listen to the truth of God's word as you fall asleep. Sing the words of God throughout your day. Listen to Christian music. You are in the process of believing the truth of who you are. You are replacing the lies of Satan with the truth of God's word. You are allowing the God of truth to *sanctify* you and transform you into the creature He created you to become.

*"For we wrestle not against flesh and blood, but against principalities, against powers, against the rulers of the darkness of this world, against spiritual wickedness in high places." Ephesians 6: 12 KJV*

*"For the weapons of our warfare are not carnal, but mighty through God to the pulling down of strongholds." 2 Corinthians 10:4 KJV*

## FEELINGS

Christ made you in his image. He created you to have many feelings and emotional expressions, just as He did. The problem comes when you use the feelings as a guide for your life and try to make sense out of feelings that are not grounded in reality and the truth of God's word. Feelings that are grounded in reality can be an indication of what you need to do.

Feelings that you tend to label in a negative way can be an indication of an ungrounded feeling. It then becomes necessary to explore: What were you thinking that caused the feeling? What event caused you to act or react in this way? (i.e.: This is the process of taking your thoughts captive to the obedience of Christ. 2 Corinthians 10:5) For example: Christ says, *"When angry, do not sin: do not ever let your wrath (your exasperation, your fury or indignation) last until the sun goes down. Leave no (such) room or foothold for the devil (give no opportunity to him)." Ephesians 4:26, 27 AMP* Christ is not condemning the emotion of anger; He is acknowledging that it is perfectly normal to have the feelings of anger. He is also cautioning you not to use your anger in a negative way to hurt or harm.

Christ talks about anger that is channeled in a positive way, when He tells you of the things that He abhors and commands you to turn away from them. (Use your anger to set a boundary). *"This know also, that in the last days perilous times shall come. For men shall be lovers of their own selves, covetous, boasters, proud, blasphemers, disobedient to parents, unthankful, unholy, without natural affection, truce breakers, false accusers, incontinent, fierce, despisers of those that are good, traitors, heady, high minded, lovers of pleasures more than lovers of God: having a form of Godliness, but denying the power thereof: from such turn away." 2 Timothy 3:1-5 KJV.*

As you become more like Him you will also abhor the things that He abhors, "RIGHTEOUS ANGER." Righteous anger can be channeled in positive ways to fight injustice, to support the weak and challenged, to drive you and motivate you to social change. It could be your anger that drives you to the very mission that Christ created, equipped, and gifted you to address. It has been our anger and the gifting(s) of God that have led us to missions that address oppression, and abuse of people both here and abroad. Christ used his anger to rid the temple of the money changers and to show his displeasure at the misuse of his temple, a place of prayer. (Anger has to be dealt with. If ignored, it causes all kinds of emotional, spiritual, and physical problems: weight gain, weight loss, high blood pressure, muscle diseases, depression, and addictions, see stage one of the model).

*"Therefore if thou bring thy gift to the altar, and there rememberest that thy brother has ought against thee; leave there thy gift before the altar, and go thy way; first be reconciled to thy brother, and then come and offer thy gift." Matthew 5:23 KJV*

On the opposite side of what you normally label a negative emotion, is what you would label a positive emotion. Explore these various emotions and ask your Heavenly Father what the positive expression of the emotion would be. You may find your mission, resolution to a problem that has plagued you for years, or guidance to explore a more positive use of the emotion. It takes all of your emotions to become whole. Feelings are healing, and they can tell you what you need.

Ask your Heavenly Father to guide you into a positive use of the emotion. Ask Him what just happened to cause you to "Feel Suspicious." Track the "negative feeling" back to the event that caused the "suspicious" feeling. What did you think about the event? Ask yourself the question: "Does my thinking line up with the word of God?" If it does not, change your thinking to match the word of God and your feelings will automatically change.

It is not an event, person, place or thing that causes you to feel a certain way. It is what you think about the event, person, place or thing that causes you to have a certain feeling. When you change what you think about the person, place or thing, your feelings will change as well. Change your feelings and your thoughts will change as well. Practice on the following examples.

**Exercise:**

Think of a "negative person" that evokes one of the "negative feelings" below. Change what you think about the person and notice how the feelings move from the "negative feelings" column to the "positive feelings" column. Notice how the action you desire to take changes with the change of your thoughts and feelings. Practice changing your negative thoughts to positive ones and notice how your feelings also move from the negative column to the positive column.

| NEGATIVE FEELINGS | POSITIVE FEELINGS |
|---|---|
| Suspicion | Trust |
| Repulsion | Attraction |
| Hurt | Relief |
| Loneliness | Community |
| Sadness | Joy |
| Anger | Affection |
| Fear | Hope |
| Weakness | Strength |
| Un- fulfilled | Satisfaction |
| Rejection | Support |
| Confusion | Clarity |

| | |
|---|---|
| Shyness | Curiosity |
| Boredom | Involvement |
| Frustration | Contentment |
| Superior | Inferior |
| Inferior | Superior |

## Prayer

*Heavenly Father, Holy Spirit I pray for wisdom and discernment as I take my thoughts captive to the obedience of Christ. I thank you Father for the living Jesus, the Holy Spirit in me that is the power to take my thoughts captive and to be obedient to your word. Write your word on the tablets of my heart that I might not sin against you.*

*Father, I thank you for all you have done in my life and all you are going to do. I thank you first of all for my salvation, that my name is written in the book of life, I thank you for the gift of your Son, His precious blood shed for my sins, I thank you for the resurrection power not only for eternal life; but also for the power to sanctify me, heal me and transform my life. Make me into the creature that you created me to become. Make me the fragrance of Christ to those that are perishing. I will give all praise and glory to you Father. It is in the name of Jesus that I pray. Amen*

## Exercise:

Think of a recent event that caused you to have what you would label "negative feeling(s)." Give the event a name. Now write down the event on the left hand column of the page, in the middle column of the page write down the thought(s) that you had about the event, on the right hand column of the page write down the feeling(s) you had about the event. Now look at the above chart. Pick out a word that most closely resembles the "negative" feeling you had. Now look at the feeling opposite the "negative" feeling.

Now go back to the column of events, thoughts and feelings on your sheet of paper. Change the thought to a positive one.

Notice how changing your thought(s), changes your feeling(s) about the event. Changing your feeling(s) about the event, changes your desires to act regarding the event. The event remains the same. It is how you think about a situation that drives your feelings. Your thoughts about the event are what make the difference in whether you view the event in a positive or negative way. Viewing an event in a positive way will cause you to have desires for positive actions in regard to the event you once viewed as negative.

Think of another event that you have negative feelings about. Proceed as before to list the event on the left hand column of the page, the thoughts about the event in the middle of the page, and the feelings about the event on the right hand column of the page.

Break up into your groups of five as before. Each person should take a turn to tell the group the event in the left hand column of the page, the thoughts about the event in the middle of the page, and the feelings about the event on the right hand column of the page.

Ask the group to tell you ways to think about the situation that are different than the way you previously thought about the event. Pick one suggestion from the group and retell your story. This time use the new thought provided by the group. Did your feelings change? How? Share with the group. Think of a time or a situation in the future when this information and exercise might benefit you. Over the next couple of days and weeks, experiment with this exercise and notice how things are different.

**THE EVENT**

_____

_____

_____

_____

_____

## THOUGHTS ABOUT THE EVENT

_____

_____

_____

_____

_____

_____

## FEELINGS ABOUT THE EVENT

_____

_____

_____

_____

_____

_____

## ACTIONS YOU TOOK IN REACTION TO THE EVENT

_____

_____

_____

_____

_____

_____

**OUTCOME OF THE EVENT**

_____

_____

_____

_____

CHANGE YOUR **THOUGHTS** ABOUT THE EVENT AND YOU CHANGE YOUR **FEELINGS** AND YOUR **ACTIONS**

NOTICE THAT THE EVENT REMAINS THE SAME. CHANGING THE THOUGHTS, CHANGES THE FEELINGS AND THE DESIRED ACTION.

**THE EVENT**

_____

_____

_____

_____

**NEW THOUGHT ABOUT THE EVENT**

_____

_____

_____

_____

**FEELINGS ABOUT THE EVENT**

_____

_____

_____

_____

_____

**ACTIONS THAT YOU COULD HAVE TAKEN**

_____

_____

_____

_____

_____

**HOW MIGHT HAVING DIFFERENT THOUGHTS, FEELINGS, AND ACTIONS HAVE CHANGED THE OUTCOME OF THE SITUATION?**

_____

_____

_____

_____

_____

_____

***Feelings that you label negative can prompt you to positive actions:***

Anger can be an indication that you need to seek protection, and set a boundary. Feelings of exhaustion can indicate a need for sanctuary, and rest. Even Jesus took time out of His day to be away from the crowds and the disciples to be alone with His Heavenly Father, and to rest.

Many times in your society men are trained to express anger; not fear or sadness. Yet Scripture tells you, *"Jesus wept." John 11:35 KJV* Women are trained to express sadness, not anger, yet Jesus expressed His anger throughout Scripture. Jesus set your example, the model to follow. Perhaps you need to examine the "traditions of men," the false teachings of your mothers, fathers, and teachers in light of examples in Scripture to restore the parts of yourself that you have left behind. If you have unexpressed and/ or unprocessed emotions and feelings, they tumble out when least expected at the most inappropriate times. Christ tells you, and cautions you *"Out of the abundance of the heart the mouth speaks." Luke 6:45 KJV*

## Example

An example of men and women and how they might handle their anger, sadness, and fear in different ways would be expressed when something negative happens. Let's say the family pet got ill and died. All family members are grieving. All have anger, sadness, and fear about the event. The male members of the family are reluctant to cry yet are very comfortable yelling at the paperboy (side-ways anger), slamming doors (side-ways anger), and blaming the vet in an accusatory tone (side-ways anger). The mom and female members of the family are more comfortable crying and expressing their sadness (They isolate and grieve alone in their separate rooms). The angry outburst of the male members just makes the situation worse and the females cry more rather than using their anger to set boundaries.

Healthy family members would all talk about their anger, use it to set boundaries and share their sadness. The healthy approach would bring family members closer for having gone through this time together. They would share their sadness, crying together and talking about how much the pet will be missed. They might share their fears that they think if they had gone to the vet sooner, the pet might have been saved. Anger that the vet could not save the pet, maybe anger expressed toward God for taking the family pet. (He is a big God. He can take it. Besides, if you have the thought, He already knows it). The healthy family talks about happy times shared with the family pet and they all express varying degrees of anger, sadness, fear and joy as they support each other through this time.

In the beginning it is probably a good idea to limit feeling identification to the four major feelings: *anger, sadness, fear, and joy*. When you are comfortable, and can easily separate your thoughts from your feelings, move on to more expressive forms of the emotions as listed below:

**ANGER:** Fury, rage, perplexed, enraged, furious, exasperated, frustrated, wrath, distressed, indignation, inflamed, irritated, agitated

**SADNESS:** Devastated, hurt, tearful, remorseful, unhappy, somber, sorrow, sorrowful, mournful, dejected, deplorable, grievous, depressed, futile, doleful

**FEAR:** Suspect, suspicion, fearful, terrified, mortified, horrified, dread, dreadful, frightful, alarming, dismay, terror, panic, afraid, perilous, dangerous, attacked, ambushed

**JOY:** Happy, joyous, jubilant, celebrating, glad, delight, thrilled, elated, pleasured, rejoice, forbearing, rejoicing, celebrate, elate, gladden, delighted, delightful, thrill

**Exercise: Expression of Feelings**

Review the list of feelings above. Identify any feelings that you either never express, or, are very uncomfortable expressing. Think back in time to when you were a child. Are there any feelings that were off limits? Not allowed. You may have been punished for expressing certain feelings. Are there any feelings that you are still uncomfortable with, as an adult? Which ones? What feelings do you express instead? For example: When you are angry, do you cry instead of expressing anger? When you are sad, do you express anger instead? Repressed feelings and/or emotions can be an indication of the kind of control that was used in your family. Record your findings below. Share with your accountability partner or small group what you discovered.

_____

_____

_____

_____

_____

_____

_____

_____

_____

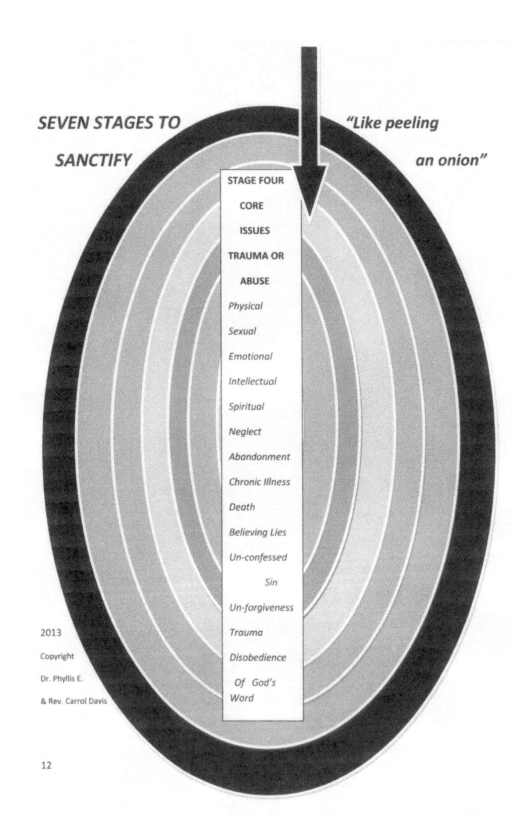

SEVEN STAGES TO SANCTIFY

"Like peeling an onion"

STAGE FOUR

CORE

ISSUES

TRAUMA OR

ABUSE

*Physical*

*Sexual*

*Emotional*

*Intellectual*

*Spiritual*

*Neglect*

*Abandonment*

*Chronic Illness*

*Death*

*Believing Lies*

*Un-confessed*

*Sin*

*Un-forgiveness*

*Trauma*

*Disobedience*

*Of God's*

*Word*

12

# Section 4:

# STAGE FOUR: DEALING WITH THE REAL ISSUES

*"If any of you lack wisdom, let him ask of God, who gives to all liberally and without reproach and it will be given to him." James 1: 5 KJV*

*C Core Issues: Trauma/Abuse*

*I admit my core issue and face the truth of my history.*

You tend to think the presenting problems, hurts, hang-ups, habits, diseases, sins, besetting sins, and addictions expressed in the beginning of your journey are the issues and if you could just solve those issues, everything would be fine. The truth is that the problems that you identified in the beginning of your journey in chapter six, stage one are just the symptoms of much deeper issues, the root problems, or core issues of your dysfunctional acting out behaviors, thoughts and feelings. It is the thoughts and feelings connected to the deeper level, core issues that drive all of the issues addressed in the first stage of the model, the presenting problems.

*The Scriptures teach about the sins of the father being passed on to the second, third, and fourth gen-erations.* (Exodus 20:5) Christ the first and divine psychologist, the *"Great Physician,"* already told you what social workers and psychologists later discovered. Disease can be biological, psychological or socio-logical in nature. That is to say that a person can inherit a gene and be predisposed to the illness. (Biology)

The problem state or disease originates in the mind: *As a man thinketh, so is he*. (Psychology / Religion): (Proverbs 23:7a) A person's surroundings and upbringing can cause and/or influence the diseased state. (Sociology) None of the above are God's will for your life, and as such we believe all to be sin and spiritual abuse, your sin or sin perpetrated against you.

At the core of the problem lie the root caus*e* and the real problem. The core issues can be physical abuse, sexual abuse, intellectual/emotional abuse, neglect, abandonment, long term illness, death or chronic illness of a family member, traumatic experiences and/or observation of any of the above issues. In processing the core events and issues you find that there are thoughts, feelings and emotions that are not in alignment with the word of God. God calls these the roots of bitterness. These are patterns that repeat in your history caused from experiencing or observing trauma and /or abuse: believing a lie(s) (from the father of lies), un- forgiveness (of God, yourself, or others), un-confessed sin, besetting sin, disobedience to God's laws (yours, or that of others). Any combination of these opens the door for Satan, the father of lies, to torture you.

Your HEAVENLY FATHER knows everything that has ever happened to you. He knows all the things that you have forgotten. He knows the things that were too traumatic to remember. He knows every interaction you have ever had and with whom you had it.

**THE PROCESS CAUTION***: When working on this part of the model, it is helpful to have a pastor, or counselor present. This part of the model can evoke very strong emotions, feelings, and body sensations. Do not attempt to do this stage of the program in a public setting, while driving or operating heavy machinery, or without professional help. Do not attempt to help a person with this process without the proper training. It is becoming a common practice for religious practitioners to claim that they can adequately guide this stage of the sanctification process. We strongly disagree. It can be extremely harmful for an unlicensed, untrained person to try to guide someone through this process. Christ told you to obey the laws of the land and to submit to authority for a reason. The law requires special training in most states to guide this process. (Romans 13:1- 4)*

*We have listed specific reasons for caution and for your consideration and discernment. "Band aid "relief can be obtained with the problem resurfacing later. Some say it will eliminate your addictions, creating false hope. The creation of false memories, the difference in directive and suggestive process is crucial and unknown by those clinically un-trained religious practitioners. There can be a lack of pacing, leading the person too rapidly, legal ramifications, breaking the dissociative barrier at inappropriate times, breaking down defenses when needed to function, failure to remove suggestive input, regression without process in all channels, (leaving the process only partially complete), premature fusion and integration, failure to recognize programming, and lack of grounding. Lack of preparation prior to abreaction can put the person at risk, failure to properly diagnose and treat the entire person. Failure to properly close the procedure can leave the person in a dissociative state, unable to function in the "here and now," safely drive, or operate machinery.*

*Many of these terms are psychological in nature and most lay persons will not understand their meaning. We write these words of caution as practiced clinician(s), licensed prayer minister(s), ordained minister(s), and biblical counselor(s) who love the Lord and want to see all of His people healed. Violation of these principles can cause extreme illness, emotional relapse, and even death. One would not go to someone for brain surgery just because that person happens to have a knife, and we suggest you treat your spiritual health and emotional well being with the same discernment. Example(s) of such problem(s) could occur if a practicing alcoholic were told they could now drink after some of the work of the sanctification process, only to relapse into a state that was worse than the previous one. People trained in the addictions field know that addiction can be arrested and treated, not cured. They would never encourage a practicing alcoholic in the sanctification process to drink, nor does the word of God. (Proverbs 23:29-31) Not only is it not OK for an alcoholic to drink or a drug addict to use. Relapse could be deadly.*

*To eliminate the defenses an individual has developed to survive, without the knowledge of what protection the defense afforded, could leave a person vulnerable to harm. One such example is in a family system of violence and spousal abuse. The defenses of lying, weight gain, manipulation etc. may serve to protect the person from harm until they are in a safe place to process the memories.*

*Working with a trained professional, who is aware of the cautions to be adhered to, will protect you from harm and provide a safe place to do this work. Wise pastors, teachers, laypersons and Bible scholars will know when they are over their heads and will refer to a professional clinician or licensed counselor trained in this particular discipline, not someone that has had a few courses and is accountable to no one for the outcome of their work.*

## THE PROCESS

**Preparation:** Prior to beginning the process, make sure that the person is in a safe place, not just for the process, but afterwards on returning home. Make sure the person has a strong support network of friends, family, church affiliation, a sponsor, accountability person, or prayer warrior. Know the background of the individual, the history: spiritual, psychological and medical and act accordingly to cover all areas in the preparation process: i.e.: What medications is the person taking? What are the telephone numbers for the support persons? It is a good idea to have someone else drive the individual to this session. Make notes, and or tape the session.

Jesus taught the disciples to bind up the "Strongman" in *Matthew 16:19 KJV: "and I will give unto thee the keys of the kingdom of Heaven: and whatsoever thou shall bind on earth shall be bound in Heaven: and whatsoever thou shall loose on earth shall be loosed in Heaven."*

## Prayer

*Bind up the enemy: An example would be: "Spirit(s) of Destruction, Demonic Spirits, Spirit(s) of confusion, I bind you in Jesus name. You will not stop, block, confuse, limit, or interfere in anyway with the gifts the true Lord Jesus has for _____ today. If you choose to speak, you will speak only what the True Lord Jesus allows you to speak, and then it will only be to reveal your presence, then you will be commanded to go to the feet of Jesus, who has authority over Heaven and earth." Amen*

*The Actual Process*

When you have a negative feeling, thought, or body sensation that you can not explain, all you have to do is to ask your Heavenly Father, Holy Spirit, to take you back to the very first time you had this negative feeling (emotional feeling and/or body sensation) and He will take you there. You can ask Him to show you what it is that He is trying to teach you, so that you can be free of the bondage created by this particular negative emotion. (Emotions are neither negative nor positive; you have labeled them as such because you as human beings tend to do so. All emotions are from God. He made you in His image. You just need to learn to channel your emotions in a positive way. On the opposite side of a negative emotion is a positive use of the energy. See the list of emotional expressions in the earlier section on feelings.)

When your Heavenly Father, Holy Spirit takes you back to a particular event, person, place, or thing, *flush out the memory*. This means to notice everything that you hear, see and feel going on inside and outside your body. Notice if there is color or black and white. Are you inside or outside? Is it hot or cold? What time of year is it? Do you recognize where you are? How old are you? What are you wearing? Who is with you? What are you doing? The more information you can get the better. The memory will usually flood with emotion. Write down everything you remember in a journal afterwards.

After the memory work, your feeling is now grounded in reality. You know exactly why you have been having the feeling, even though there is no connection to the here and now.

The original "acting out" behavior will now make sense in light of the new information uncovered. The more we hear others' stories, walk with them on their journeys, and the *sanctification* process, the more we understand, but for the grace of God, there we go.

Paul tells you to leave your past behind and to move toward your future in Christ Jesus:

*"Brethren I count not myself to have apprehended; but this one thing I do, forgetting those thing which are behind and reaching forth unto those things which are before. I press toward the mark for the prize of the high calling of God in Christ Jesus." Philippians 3:13, 14 KJV*

When able to do so, that is the best thing for you. However many times you are unable to move toward your future because something from the past has trapped your emotions. You have no idea what, and cannot let go. It is during these times when you cannot let go, that your past becomes your present and your future. You must take action to clear out the negative emotion(s) and the thoughts that are not of God, but of the enemy. We have a saying that we use to help guide our own process and that of fellow travelers, *"Whenever the feeling(s) is bigger than the event, it is always about your history."* You might think it is about something that just happened or something that was said to you; however, if the feeling is bigger than the event, we believe you are dealing with an issue out of your past.

### *Complete the Process*

It becomes necessary to fully complete the process. All of the thoughts and feelings need to be explored around the event being processed (e.g. the body sensations, negative thoughts or feelings). The person needs to be taken to a time in the future when the same event(s) might trigger the negative feelings and make sure the outcome is different. If the outcome is not different in the future, something is left to be resolved. The memory is not thoroughly processed. The person is in a dangerous place, if left there. The event can continue to process later; but closure is needed so the process does not continue as the person leaves.

### Example:

Over the next couple of hours, days and weeks your brain will continue to remember events and feelings around this process that the Lord Jesus wishes to sanctify. Write down any thoughts and feelings about the event for discussion the next time. This is not something to discuss outside of training or with an accountability person or prayer minister until the process is complete and the trainer has advised you that it is OK to proceed.

**Prayer**

*Holy Spirit, Heavenly Father I pray for your protection over_____. I pray that the defenses used to keep _____safe, stay firmly in place. I pray that your company of angels will surround them, go before and behind them to guard them in all their ways. I pray that you surround them in your white light of healing and continue the process only at the rate and speed that you deem appropriate in the process of dreaming and sleeping. Father, I ask you to surround this memory in your white light of protection until safe to process it again. I pray that if there is any physical pain associated with this memory, you will spread it over the next thousand years and that I receive only a hint of the experience in order to understand what you wish to heal. In Jesus name I pray. Amen*

The event needs to be "reframed." The missing truth, emotion, ego strength needs to be reinforced at this level prior to forgiveness. The adult needs to comfort the child within. Truth needs to be spoken to the lies, forgiveness work need to be done, vows and oaths broken, sin confessed and dealt with, sexual sin needs to be severed from the sexual partner. *"Flee fornication. Every sin that a man doeth is without the body; but he that committeth fornication, sinneth against his own body." 1 Corinthians 6:18 KJV (See forgiveness work)*

### *Closure*

Closure is necessary when taking someone back in time to a memory they have forgotten. These memories are stored in a different part of the brain than the conscious things you do in the "here" and "now." Lack of proper closure can leave a person in a dissociative state, making it unsafe to operate a car, drive, etc. Make sure the person is grounded in reality, fully back to the present, before leaving them alone.

Issues that need to be processed are: any lies, roots of bitterness, vows and oaths, sins of self, others, and un-forgiveness. These specific issues are addressed below. Exercises that can be done by the individual to address each issue are also listed:

**LIES**: Many times you believe a lie from the pit of hell, the evil one. You believe something to be true and act as if it were true. The enemy has deceived you into believing something that is not true. He comes to steal, kill and destroy and deception is his biggest tool.

**Exercise**

In this case you need to denounce the lie and replace the lie of Satan with the living, breathing word of God, His truth. Because you have believed the lie for so long and unconsciously repeated it to your brain, you need to speak the truth on a regular basis.

Post the Scriptures on post-it notes of different colors throughout your house and read the Scriptures out loud to yourself as you go about your daily chores. It takes hearing the positive Scriptures messages more than twenty times the number of times you have heard the "lies" of Satan to replace the negative messages. You want the *word of God* to surface the next time you are *"triggered,"* not the *lies of Satan*, the father of all lies.

Record your voice on a tape recorder with the truth of the word of God on the tape. Play the tape for yourself at night when you go to sleep. The truth of God will go to the same part of the brain where the lie was stored, the unconscious mind. You will be well on your way to programming your mind with the truth of God.

**ROOTS OF BITTERNESS**: Roots of bitterness are caused by intergenerational sins or addictions, physical, mental, sexual, emotional and spiritual abuse, neglect, abandonment, involvement in or witnessing a traumatic event, death or long term illness in the family and extreme loss.

Sometimes there is a traumatic event that has happened to you, something that you had long since forgotten. We believe this is God's way to protect you from the horrors of this world until you are in a safe place to process or remember what has happened to you. Then and only then will He allow you to remember. If a traumatic event is what is behind your negative emotion(s), thought(s) and behavior(s), you must forgive the person that hurt you. *"and when ye stand praying, forgive, if ye have ought against any: that your Father also which is in heaven may forgive you your trespasses. But, if you do not forgive, neither will your Father which is in heaven forgive your trespasses." Mark 11:25, 26 KJV*

However, before you can begin the forgiveness process, you must acknowledge what has happened to you. Have compassion for the child inside that remembers and endured what happened. Acknowledge the feelings, emotions and thoughts that you had about the particular incident. Acknowledge ways that the repressed memory and emotions have been driving your life, causing problems for you in very specific ways. Once the memory is thoroughly processed, then and only then should you go on to the forgiveness process.

**Exercise**

Use a journal to write down the specific event at the core or root of your issues. Write down all you can remember about the event: Who was there? What were you wearing? How old were you? Where were you? What was the weather like? What was the time of year? Was it hot or cold? What were you doing? Write as much detail as possible. What did you see? What did you hear? What did you feel? What emotional response did you have to the event? If others were present, what was their emotional response? What did you hear inside your head? What sounds did you hear around you? Did you smell anything? What did you smell? Again, give as much detail as possible about the event.

_____

_____

_____

_____

_____

_____

_____

Next, write down any thoughts that you had and anything you said. Write down the words you heard from others, if others were present. What did you say? Be sure that you list what you saw, heard, and felt: both inside you and going on around you. Were you looking out of your eyes, or, were you looking at yourself? If you were looking at yourself, were you looking down as if from the ceiling? Were you looking up from the floor? Were you looking at yourself at eye level? Be sure to write down your thoughts and feelings about the event.

_____

_____

_____

_____

_____

_____

_____

Next write down how the event has affected you in the present. Make sure you make a note of any feelings that you had: anger, sadness, fear, resentment, confusion, as well as tactile feelings, and body sensations. Make a note of your thoughts about each event that happened.

_____

_____

_____

_____

_____

_____

Make notes of what you missed as a result of the event. Make notes of the connection to the present day. Have you been repeating the trauma in some way? Have you been repeating the experience as the victim? Have you been acting out the abuser's role? What about in your relationships, your love life, your marriage? Have you been acting out your thoughts and feelings about this event and the person(s) that hurt you? Have you been reacting to the event in the here and now? When the memory is thoroughly processed you are ready for the next step:

_____

_____

_____

_____

_____

_____

_____

_____

_____

_____

The core issue could become a *"bitter root."* In Hebrews 12:5 Scripture warns about allowing bitter roots to spring up. When the core issue becomes a bitter root you can see the pattern repeated in the person's history. When the Holy Spirit takes you back to the event, memories, or circumstances causing the problem, make sure that you have gone back to the earliest time. If bitter roots have set in, you may have many similar episodes that need to be processed. Going back to the earliest memory flips the emotions, thoughts and feelings that were processed across time and you will not have to repeat the process for each single issue. If the Holy Spirit takes you to more than one issue of a similar nature, it is for a reason. There is something different about the seemingly similar events that needs to be processed as well. Do you have more than one issue to process regarding this event? Do you see a repetitive pattern in your history? Have you continued to repeat your history as the victim...the perpetrator? Record your findings below.

_____

_____

_____

_____

_____

_____

_____

On occasion, a person will see only black. They will hear nothing, and feel nothing. If this happens, do not attempt to process this particular memory without the help of a trained counselor. The experience of seeing "black" is for a reason. For the persons protection, let someone experienced in regression work help you. If after several attempts you get nothing. Have the person make notes in their journal and take the notes of the process to a trained professional. (Seeing "black" can indicate satanic involvement, confusion, or an amnesic block necessary for the person to function). Make notes of your experience below.

_____

_____

_____

_____

_____

_____

_____

**UNFORGIVENESS**: *Forgiveness does not mean that what happened to you is OK.* Forgiving someone does not mean that you allow them to repeat the process. Boundaries may need to be put in place to protect you in the future. Forgiving only means that you follow God's command to forgive. *Forgiveness is a choice, a decision of the will.* It is not a feeling, it is an action. The person no longer owes you anything. *Forgiveness is agreeing to accept the consequences of another's actions.* You release them to God's perfect justice. You recognize that they are not in God's will at the time, and that they did not know what they were doing, or they never would have committed the act. If they had the mind of Christ, their behavior would reflect the same. *"Father, forgive them for they know not what they do,"* Jesus' words on the cross as He referred to those who persecuted Him. *Forgiveness is choosing not to hold the action against them anymore.* Scriptures talk about the heart of a matter. Remembering the pain of the transgression, how it made you feel, what you thought at the time, and the effects on your life all have to be addressed in the forgiveness process. *Forgiveness needs to be from the heart in order to be complete.*

Next, you need to ask God to forgive you for your un-forgiveness, for your disobedience to His word and for letting the sun go down on your anger. Un-forgiveness opens the door for much sin and demonic spirits. Once the forgiveness has taken place, you can announce to any demonic spirits that they must flee. *"So be subject to God, resist the devil (that is stand firm against him) and he will flee from you."* James *4:7 AMP* They no longer have any authority to be there, they must go. As you command the demon spirits to go, ask the Lord Jesus to fill you up with the white light of His protection and healing.

**Exercise(s):**

The forgiveness process can be done in several ways:

**Exercise: Empty Chair Technique** requires the presence of a sponsor, pastor, counselor, and or a trained clinician.

Place an empty chair approximately 12 feet in front of you, facing you. Imagine the person that you need to forgive sitting in the chair. Describe them in detail: what they are wearing, their body posture, the look on their face, and the sound of their voice. You may need someone to stand behind the chair to be certain the person stays in the chair. (We know that sounds strange, but trust us, it can help encourage and support you to have a partner as you do this exercise). This work is to be done from the heart of the memory, the thoughts and feelings of the child that was harmed, not the logical, rational adult mind of reason; but from the child's point of view.

Look at the notes from the previous exercise and tell the person what you think and how you feel about the event. Let them know how the event affected you. Tell them, "I'm angry with you," "I'm sad about what you did or said." Express all of your thoughts and feelings about what happened to you. Let Christ and your adult /self stand -up for the little child inside, that was not protected. Acknowledge how long the "child inside" has held the memory until it was safe to remember. Thank the "child inside" and acknowledge the strength and courage that it took to hold on to the memory.

Next tell the perpetrator that you did not deserve what happened and you are holding them accountable. If you carry "shame" about the event, give it back to them. Tell them it does not belong to you because you did nothing wrong. The "shame" belongs to them. Let them know how what they did has affected your entire life. Let them know how you feel and what you think about that. Once the memory is thoroughly processed, move on to the forgiveness stage.

Tell them you forgive them for what they did because Christ commands you to, not because they deserve it, and not because what they did was OK. Tell them you release them to God's perfect justice, in obedience to Christ.

Next ask God to forgive you. Ask Him to forgive you for your un-forgiveness, for letting the sun go down on your anger, for not following His word. Ask Him to fill you with healing and protection.

Next command any demonic spirits to leave. They no longer have authority to be there. You have forgiven your perpetrator, you have asked God to forgive you, and they must flee.

Imagine a time in the future when a similar situation might happen and notice how it is different. Describe what you see, hear and feel. (If the future is not different, the memory is not thoroughly processed and you need to continue as before: Ask your Heavenly Father, Holy Spirit what else you need to remember, what else do you need to see, hear or feel to release this event? Ask Him to take you there, and you will follow).

Next, ask your Heavenly Father, the Holy Spirit to fill you with truth and his healing energy. Ask Him to replace all of the "negativity" with the "positive" energy of his white light of healing.

**Exercise: Journal Work**

This is the same process as above, except that the event, thoughts and feelings are written down to be processed later, when read aloud to a sponsor, pastor, mentor, or counselor specifically trained to do this type of work.

**Exercise: Letter *DO NOT MAIL IT***

The use of a letter to write down your thoughts, feelings and how you have been affected in a letter to your perpetrator can be very healing, allowing for closure in a safe way. It is to be read to your sponsor, pastor, mentor, or counselor. It is not to be mailed; but is for you to process the event. Do not mail it unless advised to do so by an experienced counselor. *"He who rebukes a scorner, heaps upon himself abuse, and he who reproves a wicked man gets for himself bruises. Reprove not a scorer, lest he hate you." Proverbs 9: 7, 8 KJV*

**Exercise: Break the bond created by sexual sin**

Imagine a cord that runs between yourself and the person with whom you committed sexual sin. Imagine the cord (connection) being severed. Watch as they drift away from you. Wish them well as they depart. (To be done after the forgiveness work. Include your former partner, and yourself. Be sure to seek God's forgiveness for the sins against his Holy temple, your body).

**VOWS and OATHS:** It could be a vow or an oath. Scripture says that *"When you make a vow to the Lord, you shall not be slack in paying it, for the Lord your God will surely require it of you, and slackness would be sin in you. If you refrain from vowing, it will not be sin in you."* Deut. 23: 21, 22 KJV. A vow to tithe to the Church goes unfulfilled and is a sin that must be confessed. The vow or oath could be to an organization, in a membership charter or to a person. It could be a vow or an oath that you made to yourself. An example of such a vow or an oath would be:

A vow or promise to an organization such as: satanic cults, religious cults, sects, the rituals and membership requirements of rush week in some fraternities, sororities, secretive organizations, some court proceedings, and even some churches. (Members of some organizations make a vow and or oath to lie if necessary, in a court of law, to protect its members, in direct opposition to the word of God). *"Thou shalt not bear false witness against thy neighbor."* 10 Commandments

*"Again ye have heard that it hath been said by them of old time, thou shalt not foreswear thyself, but shall perform unto the Lord thine oaths: But I say unto you, swear not at all; neither by heaven; for it is God's throne: nor by the earth; for it is His footstool: neither by Jerusalem; for it the city of the great King. Neither shalt thou swear by thy head, because thou canst not make one hair white or black. But let your communication be. Yea, yea: Nay, nay: for whatsoever is more than these cometh of evil."* Matthew 5:33-37 KJV

Sometimes you make declarations to yourselves. You use *generalizations* to disavow the truth when you use expressions such as: I'll *never, have to, must, can not, always, only.* There is no room for an exception to the rule, and you trap yourself in your own deceit until you disavow the statement. Example: "I'll never depend on a man for my livelihood," traps you into fulfilling your own prophecy because you have made a vow or an oath in direct contradiction to God's word: *"If a man vow a vow unto the Lord, or swear an oath to bind his soul with a bond; He shall not break his word. He shall do according to all that proceeded out of his mouth. Numbers 30:2 KJV* You are commanded not to take the Lord's name in vain; to do so binds your soul: Cussing, foul language, vulgar talk is not of God.

*"And ye shall not swear by my name falsely, neither shalt thou profane the name of thy God: I am the Lord."* Leviticus 19:12 KJV

The Lord Jesus requires you to make vows to no one except the Lord. If you have made such a vow or oath the remedy is to disavow the vow or oath and to replace it with a vow only to the Lord Jesus Christ. It is also necessary to ask for forgiveness for not following the word of God. *"You shall not make a vow or oath except unto the Lord." Matthew 5:33-37 KJV* Scripture teaches you to disavow oaths and vows in *Matthew 5:33-37 KJV. "When you make a vow to the Lord, you shall not be slack in paying it, for the Lord your God will surely require it of you and slackness would be a sin in you. If you refrain from vowing it will not be sin in you."*

In other words, be a person of your word. Honestly report the truth of a situation. Let your integrity stand for itself....Let your "yes" mean "yes" and your "no" mean "no." Teach people through their dealings with you, that you speak the truth as you know it to be, that you can be relied on to speak honestly, and that your word is your bond without oaths or promises, because of your commitment to Christ.

## SINS of SELF and OTHERS

You are taught to repent of your sin and turn from your sin in the Scriptures. You are also taught that if you belong to Christ you are forgiven of your sin(s). Christ paid the debt, He did not owe, with his blood, when He died for your sin(s), past, present and future. We must confess our sin and turn from our wicked ways. (Ezekiel 33:11; 2 Kings 17:13) and we must confess our sins to one another so that we may heal. (James 5:16)

Scripture also talks about the sins of the father handed down to the second, third and fourth generation. (Exodus 20:5) Examples of the bitter root would be found in the home of the alcoholic, drug addict, sex addict, co-dependent, gambling addict, rage a holic, work- a -holic, etc. Any addiction in the home can cause bitter roots to form in its family members. Identify any addictive behaviors and attitudes in your family of origin and steer clear. Psychologists have known for years that there is more to addiction than just partaking of the substance. There is a whole socialization around addiction in the form of attitudes and behaviors that are dysfunctional and ungodly that will lead you down a path of destruction. The Lord promises that *"When your mother and father betray you, He will lift you up." Psalms 27:10 KJV* He further instructs you to *"Work out your salvation with fear and trembling." Philippians 2:12 KJV* Esau gave up his inheritance for a bowl of soup. Jacob was a liar and deceiver filled with jealousy and envy (Genesis 25:28-34). Both are biblical examples of bitter root and sin, and disobedience to God's word. Scripture cautions you to *"Resist the devil and he will flee from you." James 4:7 KJV* and in 2 *Corinthians 10:6 KJV* you are told to *"take our thoughts captive to the obedience of Christ."*

Early childhood trauma can cause an adult to be trapped in the memory of the past without a conscious awareness. The child/now adult acts out the abuse as the victim(s) or the perpetrator(s) of the original offense. Scripture warns you of such things and cautions you not to let *"bitter roots spring up." Hebrews 12:5 KJV*

Physical abuse is the last stage in acting out violence against women and children. The physical abuse starts with false beliefs that drive negative emotions, followed by physical abuse. Intellectual and emotional abuses precede the violence of physical abuse and murder. South Carolina has ranked in the top ten in the nation for violence against women for the past fifteen years. One in four women in the United States will become a victim of criminal domestic violence in their lifetime.

The "traditions of men," cultural norms, and the socialization of people in some parts of the country encourage this trend. Failure to recognize and stop abuse at the less threatening levels allows it to escalate. Emotional and intellectual abuse precedes the later, more violent stage of murder, and can be challenged more easily. Learning what intellectual and emotional abuse is can change long established traditions and cultural norms that do not line up with the word of God. Most men in violent relationships have not been taught to respect women as their equal and fellow heirs to the throne of God. The Bible and Scriptures are distorted to reflect a "less than mentality."

## *Prejudice*

In stage two of the model, you discovered some of the defenses that lead to these statistics: discounting, blame-frame, minimizing, denial, delusion, rapid speech, anger, fidgeting, laughing, side-ways anger/sarcasm, busy, isolating/withdrawing, distracting, labeling, generalizations, name calling, mind games, rationalization/justification, manipulation, and lies. Exploring these unhealthy character traits will allow you to set appropriate boundaries and change these statistics, changing your behavior to reflect the "Mind of Christ" rather than the "Lies of Satan." In the South, with a church on almost every corner, there is no excuse for the lack of training and education that would most likely change these statistics and the attitude(s) of men and women toward women in this part of the country. We mention women and their attitudes and traditions along with men because the women help to uphold the dysfunction by allowing the abuse, failure to set boundaries, not knowing who they are in Christ, failure to flag abusive attitudes, beliefs, and actions, failure to know and flag intellectual, emotional, physical and spiritual abuse. Lack of awareness in men and women, the cultural norms, and sometimes spiritual teaching and distortion of the Scriptures help to foster abuse and the alarming statistics reflected in some parts of the country.

Scripture says that you will be held accountable for your actions and inactions. Treating women as Christ would is part of the discipleship and training you are called by Christ himself to teach in *"The Great Commission."*

Remember that you have issues, you are on your own individual journeys and many people provide inaccurate information through the filters of their own dysfunctional history. You can use your own dysfunctional upbringing and the *"traditions of men"* to distort the word of God and prevent rightly applying the word of God.

Misapplication of God's word can be a form of spiritual, intellectual, emotional, and physical abuse. Wars have been fought in the name of the Lord, when God had nothing to do with the issues. Women have been killed and children murdered in the name of the Lord and with the rationalization and justification of the Scriptures' teachings when the word of God is distorted.

*"There is a way which seemeth right unto a man, but the end thereof are the ways of death." Proverbs 14:12 KJV* In *James 4: 7 KJV* the Bible teaches you to *"Resist the devil and he will flee from you."* Satan, the father of *Lies* uses deceptive methods and lies to keep you from the truth. Scripture further teaches you to *"take our thoughts captive to the obedience of Christ." 2 Corinthians 10: 6 KJV*

Exploring your childhood, histories, culture and social norms can help you get in touch with any teachings, values and or beliefs that do not line up with the word of God and prevent you from enjoying the abundant life Christ died to give you. Remember that deception and lies are Satan's biggest tools for distorting the truth of God and causing you to believe his lies. He comes to steal, kill, and destroy. Below is an exercise that will help put you in touch with any inter-generational sin in your background.

**Prayer**

*Heavenly Father I pray for your wisdom and discernment. You know everything that has ever happened to me, you know all of my relatives and all of their weaknesses and shortcomings. You know every breath that I take and the numbers of hairs on my head. Your word says that I can ask you and you will be my teacher and that you will reveal to me the things I know not of. So, Father I pray that you will give me guidance and wise counsel as I do this next exercise. I pray that you will heal the brokenness in my life, moving me from glory to glory, making me more like your precious Son. It is in his name that I pray. Amen*

**Exercise: Intergenerational Sin**

In a note pad make a sheet for your mother, your father, your grandmother (maternal), your grandfather (maternal), your grandmother (paternal) and your grandfather (paternal).

On each sheet list the positive characteristic(s) for each family member on their page on the right hand side column. List that family member's negative character traits on the left hand side of the page. Do this for each family member.

Now make the same kind of list for each serious relationship you have been in. Make one for steady boyfriends and/or girlfriends, persons you were engaged to, marital partners (prior) and (present).

Next make a sheet for yourself. Put the character traits that you consider to be positive on the right side of the page, in the right hand column. Put the negative character traits on the left hand side of the page, and in the left hand column.

Now compare the list of character traits for each person with whom you have had a serious relationship and notice that the person most resembles: Mom, Dad, Grandma, Grandpa, Granny or Granddad. Make a note of your findings.

Now compare the list you made for yourself and notice whom you got your positive character traits from. Whom did you get your negative traits from? Are you most like your Mom or your Dad? Maybe you have many traits of your grandparents. Children that are raised by their grandparents will many times have more of their grandparents' traits, than the traits of their parents.

If you are from a blended family, make a sheet for each blended parental figure as well. List their positive traits in a column on the right side of the page, their negative traits on the left side of the page. Compare as before.

Notice the character traits of the persons that you have been in serious relationship with. Do they have the same or similar character traits as your Mom or your Dad? Are they negative or positive character traits? Unresolved issues from your childhood will be reflected in your choices for intimate relationships. What have you learned?

Discuss your findings with your sponsor, mentor, pastor, Bible study teacher, counselor and or a close friend whom you can trust to give you appropriate feed back. If you work a 12 Step Program, this exercise could help you with Step 4, 5, and 6. Ask your sponsor. If you are a workshop participant discuss your findings with your small group.

**Prayer**

*Heavenly Father, Holy Spirit, thank you for shinning your light in the dark and prejudice areas of my life. Father, I seek to be more like you in all I say and do. I want my life to be a reflection of the Holy Spirit shinning through me. I seek to be the fragrance of sweet perfume to all those that are perishing, so that they might see your light and be drawn to you. Father, your word says that you will give me the desires of my heart and that your word will not return void. I ask that you sanctify my thinking, help me to take my thoughts captive to the obedience of Christ. Take my heart of stone and turn it to a heart of flesh. Let what pleases you, please me. Let what is abhorrent to you; be abhorrent to me as well. Make me more like you in all I say and do. Thank you for "sanctifying" my prejudice toward _____, _____, and _____. Thank you for saving me from the worn out traditions of the past that are not in your image. Help me tear down the altars my fathers and forefathers have built. The altars of _____, _____, and _____. I will give you the praise and glory. It is in your precious Son's name that I pray, in Jesus name. Amen.*

## UNFORGIVENESS

Christ taught you to forgive everyone everything or your Heavenly Father can not forgive you. (Matthew 6:12, 14, 15. Matthew 18:21 & 35 KJV) It becomes apparent that some problems and diseases have their root(s) in many violations of God's word. You have to continue to address the issue(s) until all aspects have been processed.

There are some core issues which psychologists call *flagship issues*. This means that the issue was so traumatic that there are numerous lies, false beliefs, numerous persons, much un-forgiveness, and bitter root(s) associated with the single event.

In the example of Beatrice, the first process work might be on the smell of the beans (trigger) associated with the repressed abuse (core issue). Later in Beatrice's life she might meet a person (trigger) whom she just cannot stand for any obvious or explainable reason. In the process you find that the person's facial features resemble the mother's who stood by helplessly as Beatrice was being abused. Beatrice has anger and resentment toward the mother that did not protect her. These repressed feelings are now getting transferred to the new acquaintance without her conscious awareness or an understanding as to why she feels the way she does toward this new acquaintance.

A good way to determine if you are reacting out of reality or some repressed issue is to ask yourself: *"Is my feeling bigger than the event?"* If your feeling is bigger than the event, it is most always about your history! (Consider emotional feelings and somatic body sensations or feelings)

**Examples of Repressed Trauma**

Repressed trauma can be from something that happened to you or to someone else. Observing a traumatic event can cause repression of the event and the thoughts that accompany it. Two examples of repressed trauma follow:

*The first example is from an older gentleman we will call Gene who presents with somatic pain or body memories: The feelings were extreme, bigger than the event, in that the doctors could not find anything physically wrong. The pain sometimes kept him up at night. The breathing problem prevented normal activity, like climbing the stairs. The dizziness caused concern because it sometimes felt as if he would pass out. The process work follows using the model for each stage:*

*Stage One*: *Physical Problem(s)*: Extreme dizziness, extremely high heart rate, blood pressure was normal, body aches and pains. Prior physical exam revealed no known cause for the symptoms. Patient was being treated for high blood pressure.

*Stage Two*: *Defenses:* Rationalize and Justify, Change the subject, Minimize the response(s), thoughts and feeling(s), Dismiss the thoughts and feelings as not relevant and unimportant

*Stage Three*: *Feelings* and *Thoughts (Ungrounded)*: Terror / Fear. I see black. My body aches, rapid breathing, panicky feeling. "I don't know why. I can't explain it."

*Stage Four:* *Core Issue(s)*: Trauma, Abuse, and Violence: "I see blood...chickens...my brother's casket." "My brother's dead." "I see my Dad." "He is in a rage." "I am all alone." "I am terrified." "I am going to die." "My Dad is yelling, hitting, and angry." "I am all alone." "No one is there."(Rapid breathing, body shaking, crying, shaking head)(Feelings: Extreme Terror; Thoughts: "I am going to die.")

**Stage Five:** *Feelings: (Grounded in Reality)*.Extreme sadness, crying, body tremors Thoughts: I think my father might have killed my brother." The thoughts and feelings are connected to an event.

**Stage Six**: *Shame and Guilt Cycle*: (Denial, Delusion, Rationalize/Justify, Anger, Sadness, and Acceptance) Thoughts: "I must have made that up. Surely that could not have happened. I was terrified of him. I thought I was going to be killed just like those chickens. Could that really have happened? It must have, oh, God, no." (Acceptance follows). "Well, whether he killed him or not, I knew he was capable and he terrified me." (There is a partial resolution to the repressed memory and body sensations. More of this memory might follow).

**Stage Seven**: *He sets the captives free*. There is a partial resolution to the breathing issue, less body aches and pains. The dizziness is completely gone. Resolution of the core issue(s) frees you from bondage in this area.

*This is **your story and your testimony** of how Christ set you free from your former bondage.*

*The second example is from a man you will call "Joe" that went back to an earlier event in his history, approximately forty years before, when he was a small boy on a farm:*

Joe was a small boy working on the farm with his father. The father was driving a huge tractor with an attachment on the front designed to till the earth. As the now adult went back in time to discover the root of his problem, tremendous grief surfaced. Through his tears the adult/boy described in a "childish" voice and extreme emotions, the vision that he was remembering. His father had fallen off the tractor and under the attachment to his death. The small boy was so traumatized; he repressed the memory for over forty years. Once the memory was processed, the emotions and thoughts flipped through time and the presenting problems were no longer an issue for this man. His grief had been so severe that his personality had fractured into many persons creating much chaos in his life. i.e. Multiple Personality Disorder or what is now referred to as Identity Disorder After the remembered tragedy was processed, Joe's different personalities fused, meaning that the amnesic barrier dissolved and all of the "personalities" that were Joe, became one person.

*The third and fourth examples are from two different and necessary medical procedures; the resulting repression of the events were necessary until the now adults could deal with the issues.*

The trauma can be from a medical procedure that was traumatic to the child. Tommy had polio as a child and the treatment involved medical procedures that were very painful. The disease also called for isolation. Tommy was separated from everyone in a room all by himself. When his parents came to visit, they were wearing white gowns and white masks that scared him. As an adult looking back on the memory, we were able to explain to the child what had happened, to dispel his fears and talk to the traumatized child about his experience. The emotions and lies could be released in a controlled and safe environment.

*Sometimes the trauma can be from well intended and necessary experiences, such as the above. The child is not talked through the pain or thoughts, and the memory becomes repressed. One such incident happened to a now adult of approximately 40 years of age:*

As a little girl, Teresa suffered from a severe bladder infection. The medical procedure prescribed to rid the child of the infection was severely painful and the memory was repressed. It required going back to release the memory. Whenever the memory might include physical pain, it is necessary to space the pain over the next several days, weeks and months in order to keep the person from actually feeling the physical pain again and re-traumatizing them. All that is necessary to process the memory is a slight memory of the incident to bring forth the thoughts and feelings of the buried trauma. Inexperienced pastors, lay persons, counselors have missed this step and caused a great deal of unnecessary pain and harm by re traumatizing the individual in the process of remembering.

*Misapplication of the Scriptures by well intended parents who love their children and want the best for them can cause trauma.*

Well intended parents who love their children and want the best for their children fall victim to false scriptural teachings and cultural/traditional influences. One such issue is the notion that to "spare the rod is to spoil the child." Countless regressions to the physical abuse of a child have been at the core of repressed trauma and unresolved issues. Many times the child was not aware of why they were being "disciplined." On other occasions, the parent did not realize their strength or chose to "discipline" while still angry. Cultural norms and the way one was disciplined as a child can dictate how you discipline your children.

Physical violence of an adult toward another adult is called assault and is punishable by imprisonment. Just the threat of such violence carries a sentence in some states of five years. Physical violence toward a child is never appropriate. It is now against the law and can land a person in prison for doing so. It is a violation of trust in a person that is commissioned by God to protect and keep safe from harm. (The perpetrator can be a relative, a babysitter, a teacher, a coach, a school official, principle, or a Sunday school teacher). This action against a child can produce severe trust and intimacy issues that follow into adulthood. If the child is disrobed in the process, issues of sexual abuse must be processed as well.

*"The Lord is my shepherd, I shall not want. He makes me to lie down in green pastures; He leads me beside the still waters. He restores my soul; He leads me in the paths of righteousness For His name's sake." Psalms 23:1-3* God can and will restore your soul, if you will let Him. *Praise God!*

**THE REAL ISSUES / ROOT PROBLEM / CORE ISSUES**: In summary, the root problem(s) or core issues(s) are at the bottom of the dysfunctional behavior that you are hoping God will transform and/ or *sanctify.*

At the core of the problem lie the *root cause* and the *real problem.* The *core issue(s)* can be physical abuse, sexual abuse, intellectual/emotional abuse, neglect, abandonment, long term illness, death or chronic illness of a family member, traumatic experience(s) and/or observation of any of the above issues. In processing the core events and issues you find that there are thoughts, feelings and emotions that are not in alignment with the word of God. God calls these the *root(s) of bitterness*. These are patterns that repeat in your history caused from experiencing or observing trauma and /or abuse: *believing a lie(s)* (from the father of lies), *un forgiveness* (of God, yourself, or others), *un confessed sin, besetting sin, disobedience to God's laws* (yours, or that of others). Any combination opens the door for *Satan, the father of lies,* to torture you.

Abuse is repeated in the adult/child's life as the trauma repeats. The abuse cycle is reenacted as either the victim or the perpetrator without intervention. The abuse sets the stage for broken boundaries and a repeating of the trauma by choice of life partners.

All abuse is spiritual abuse, the sins of the father in a fallen world, passed on to the second, third and fourth generation. The way the adult/child sees God and the character traits will be distorted to reflect the traits of the abuser rather than the character of God as described in the Scriptures.

The list below, (although not exhaustive) gives you an idea of what some of those issues could be. Circle any that apply to you and list them at the bottom following each category.

**PHYSICAL ABUSE**: Pinching, tickling, rough play, kicking, slapping, hitting, throwing objects, spitting, hitting with objects, dragging, shoving, twisting of the arms, legs or, body parts, burning, cutting, hair pulling, banging of head or body parts, threaten harm, shaking, restraining, locking up, put in a closed space or closet, choked, pushed, tied up, whipped, sexual conduct against another that is unwelcomed or underage, failure to provide food, shelter, clothing, medical attention, exposure to the elements, observing any of these things and refusal or inability to intervene

I believe that I was physically abused in the following ways:

1._____     7._____

2._____     8._____

3._____     9._____

4._____     10._____

5._____     11._____

6._____     12._____

Some of my negative thoughts and negative feelings resulting from my physical abuse are as follows:

NEGATIVE THOUGHTS                                 NEGATIVE FEELINGS

1._____   1._____

2._____   2._____

3._____   3._____

4._____   4._____

5._____   5._____

6._____   6._____


Some of the lies I have believed about myself as a result of my physical abuse are:

1._____   7._____

2._____   8._____

3._____   9._____

4._____   10._____

5._____   11._____

6._____   12._____


Children that are physically abused will view God and His character through the lens of their abuse. They will believe that God is mean and abusive ready to strike them if they make a mistake. They will not see God's true character as loving, gentle and protective. They have to be taught as adults that He is patient and slow to anger. (Psalm 18:2; Jeremiah 31:3; Exodus 34:6; 2 Peter 3:9)

Some of the lies I have believed about my Heavenly Father as a result of my physical abuse are:

1._____    7._____

2._____    8._____

3._____    9._____

4._____    10._____

5._____    11._____

6._____    12._____

**EMOTIONAL ABUSE:** Name calling, belittling, refusing to let one express all of their emotions, calling a person their behavior, deny a persons' feelings, isolate, mistreat, discounting a person or their achievements, minimizing the accomplishments/ achievements of another, discounting fears, failures, and problems, refusing to render aid, observing the above and refusing to act or intervene. Circle any of the above that apply to you and list them below.

I believe that I was emotionally abused in the following ways:

1._____    7._____

2._____    8._____

3._____    9._____

4._____    10._____

5._____    11._____

6._____    12._____

Some of my negative thoughts and negative feelings resulting from my emotional abuse are as follows:

NEGATIVE THOUGHTS                NEGATIVE FEELINGS

1._____    1._____

2._____    2._____

3._____    3._____

4._____    4._____

5._____    5._____

6._____    6._____

Some of the lies I have believed about myself as a result of my emotional abuse are:

1._____    7._____

2._____    8._____

3._____    9._____

4._____    10._____

5._____    11._____

6._____    12._____

Children that are emotionally abused will see God through the lens of their abuse. They will believe that God is distant, disinterested, absent, insensitive and uncaring. They will have to reprogram their mind with the truth from God's word about His character. God is involved in your life. He wants an intimate relationship with you. His kindness and compassion never fail. You are the apple of His eye. (Deuteronomy 32:9, 10)

Some of the lies I have believed about my Heavenly Father as a result of my emotional abuse are:

1._____    7._____

2._____    8._____

3._____    9._____

4._____    10._____

5._____    11._____

6._____    12._____

**INTELLECTUAL ABUSE**: Name calling, belittling, telling one they are their negative behavior, ignoring, refusing to speak to /or communicate with, labeling individuals, generalizing individuals, treat like objects instead of people, discounting ideas and thoughts, ignoring, failure to teach or educate a child, failure to socialize a child, observing the same and refusing to act or intervene. Circle any that apply to you and your life and list them below.

I believe that I was intellectually abused in the following ways:

1._____   7._____

2._____   8._____

3._____   9._____

4._____   10._____

5._____   11._____

6._____   12._____

Some of my negative thoughts and negative feelings resulting from my intellectual abuse are as follows:

NEGATIVE THOUGHTS                NEGATIVE FEELINGS

1._____   1._____

2._____   2._____

3._____   3._____

4._____   4._____

5._____   5._____

6._____   6._____

Some of the lies I have believed about myself as a result of my intellectual abuse are:

1._____   7._____

2._____   8._____

3._____   9._____

4._____   10._____

5._____   11._____

6._____   12._____

Children that are intellectually abused will grow up to see their Heavenly Father through the lens of the abusive parent's character traits. They will have to reprogram their mind to believe the truth of God's character as accepting, committed to your growth, plans for your future to prosper you; not to harm you, to give you hope and a future. (Jeremiah 29:11; Romans 15:7; Luke 15:11-16; Hebrews 4:15, 16)

Some of the lies I have believed about my Heavenly Father as a result of my intellectual abuse are:

1._____    7._____

2._____    8._____

3._____    9._____

4._____    10._____

5._____    11._____

6._____    12._____

**SEXUAL ABUSE:** Rape, incest, fornication, adultery, sodomy, touching one in a sexual and inappropriate way, sexual comments, comments about ones body, weight gain/loss, disrobing a child to spank them, physical abuse of the face, homosexuality, sexually perverse acts, bestiality, pornography, sex with the dead, preferential treatment of one gender over another i.e. preference to males and favor to; or preference and favoritism to females , forced sexual acts, children exposed to sex and sexual behavior prior to the age of consent, adults disrobing, bathing, and/ or sleeping with children, exposure of the adult body parts to children, lack of privacy when using the toilet and bathing, observing the same and refusal and/ or inability to render aid. Circle any of the above that apply to you and list them below.

I believe that I was sexually abused in the following ways:

1._____    7._____

2._____    8._____

3._____    9._____

4._____    10._____

5._____    11._____

6._____    12._____

Some of my negative thoughts and negative feelings resulting from my sexual abuse are as follows:

NEGATIVE THOUGHTS          NEGATIVE FEELINGS

1._____  1._____

2._____  2._____

3._____  3._____

4._____  4._____

5._____  5._____

6._____  6._____

Some of the lies I have believed about myself as a result of my sexual abuse are:

1._____  7._____

2._____  8._____

3._____  9._____

4._____  10._____

5._____  11._____

6._____  12._____

Children that are sexually abused will grow up to see God's character through the lens of their abuse. They will believe that God is not trustworthy, protective, kind, nor compassionate. The adult has to re-program the mind to the truth of God's character through the word of God. (Hosea 11: 3, 4; Jeremiah 31:3; Psalms 18:2)

Some of the lies I have believed about my Heavenly Father as a result of my sexual abuse are:

1._____  7._____

2._____  8._____

3._____  9._____

4._____  10._____

5._____  11._____

6._____  12._____

**NEGLECT:** Failure to provide food, shelter, clothing, medical attention, teaching, nurturing, encouragement, rules and consequences, failure to discipline, observation of these issues without intervention.

I believe that I was abused by neglect in the following ways:

1._____     7._____

2._____     8._____

3._____     9._____

4._____     10._____

5._____     11._____

6._____     12._____

Some of my negative thoughts and negative feelings resulting from the abuse of neglect are as follows:

NEGATIVE THOUGHTS               NEGATIVE FEELINGS

1._____     1._____

2._____     2._____

3._____     3._____

4._____     4._____

5._____     5._____

6._____     6._____

Some of the lies I have believed about myself as a result of the abuse of neglect are:

1._____     7._____

2._____     8._____

3._____     9._____

4._____     10._____

5._____     11._____

6._____     12._____

Adults that were neglected as children believe that God will neglect them. They suffer from abandonment issues and repeat the cycle of their childhood abuse in their adult lives. They have to reprogram their minds with the truth of God's character as always with them, and will never leave them. They have to re-teach themselves of His provision, love and protection. They have to be told that if it is important to them, it is important to God. (Hebrews 13:5; Isaiah 40:11; John 10:10)

Some of the lies I have believed about my Heavenly Father as a result of neglect are as follows:

| | |
|---|---|
| 1._____ | 7._____ |
| 2._____ | 8._____ |
| 3._____ | 9._____ |
| 4._____ | 10._____ |
| 5._____ | 11._____ |
| 6._____ | 12._____ |

**ABANDONMENT**: Physically, intellectually, emotionally, spiritually left alone, failure to be there physically, emotionally, intellectually, or spiritually for a child (A parent can be there physically and spaced out or otherwise distracted and not there in the mind), observation of these issues and refusal to intervene. Circle any above that apply to you and list below.

I believe that I was abused by abandonment in the following ways:

| | |
|---|---|
| 1._____ | 7._____ |
| 2._____ | 8._____ |
| 3._____ | 9._____ |
| 4._____ | 10._____ |
| 5._____ | 11._____ |
| 6._____ | 12._____ |

Some of my negative thoughts and negative feelings resulting from the abuse of abandonment are as follows:

NEGATIVE THOUGHTS                                    NEGATIVE FEELINGS

1._____          1._____

2._____          2._____

3._____          3._____

4._____          4._____

5._____          5._____

6._____          6._____

Some of the lies I have believed about myself as a result of the abuse of abandonment are:

1._____          7._____

2._____          8._____

3._____          9._____

4._____          10._____

5._____          11._____

6._____          12._____

Children abandoned by their care givers believe that God will also abandon them. Trust is hard for them and they have to repeat the Words of God's character. They have to take baby steps in order to learn that God is trustworthy. (Lamentations 3:22, 23; Ezekiel 34:11-16)

Some of the lies I have believed about my Heavenly Father as a result of my abandonment are as follows:

1._____          7._____

2._____          8._____

3._____          9._____

4._____          10._____

5._____          11._____

6._____          12._____

**CHRONIC, LONG TERM ILLNESS:** Your long term illness or that of a family member takes away from the family balance and causes issues of aloneness, confusion, fear, neglect, and abandonment as well as some of the aforementioned problems, refusal or inability to intervene. Circle any of the above that apply to you and list them below.

I believe that my/or my family member's chronic and/or long term illness affected me in the following ways:

1._____     7._____
2._____     8._____
3._____     9._____
4._____     10._____
5._____     11._____
6._____     12._____

Some of my negative thoughts and negative feelings resulting from illness are as follows:

NEGATIVE THOUGHTS                  NEGATIVE FEELINGS

1._____     1._____
2._____     2._____
3._____     3._____
4._____     4._____
5._____     5._____
6._____     6._____

Some of the lies I have believed about myself as a result of the chronic/long term illness are as follows:

1._____     7._____
2._____     8._____
3._____     9._____
4._____     10._____
5._____     11._____
6._____     12._____

Children that grew up with long term illness and or death fear death and destruction and do not trust God to protect them. They need to reprogram their minds to the truth of the word of God. They need to know that He alone determines the day of their birth and the hour of their death. He knew them before the world began.

Some of the lies I have believed about my Heavenly Father as a result of chronic/long term illness are as follows:

1._____     7._____
2._____     8._____
3._____     9._____
4._____     10._____
5._____     11._____
6._____     12._____

**DEATH:** Can cause issues of aloneness, abandonment, shame, fear, neglect, and a sense of failure as well as the above mentioned issues, failure to understand and communicate the experience, observation without ability to intervene. Circle all that apply to you and list them below.

I believe that (my friend's name/or my family member's name) _____ death affected me in the following ways:

1._____     7._____
2._____     8._____
3._____     9._____
4._____     10._____
5._____     11._____
6._____     12._____

Some of my negative thoughts and negative feelings resulting from _____death are as

follows:

NEGATIVE THOUGHTS                          NEGATIVE FEELINGS

1._____          1._____

2._____          2._____

3._____          3._____

4._____          4._____

5._____          5._____

6._____          6._____


Some of the lies I have believed about myself as a result of _____ death are as

follows:

1._____          7._____

2._____          8._____

3._____          9._____

4._____          10._____

5._____          11._____

6._____          12._____

Children that grew up with issues of death, abandonment, fear and rejection do not understand nor

comprehend a God that offers protection, provision and eternal life. The adult has to diligently pursue

the truth of God's character and eternal life. The adult/child needs to know that no one can snatch them

out of God's hand.

Some of the lies I have believed about my Heavenly Father as a result of _____ death are as follows:

1._____     7._____

2._____     8._____

3._____     9._____

4._____     10._____

5._____     11._____

6._____     12._____

**TRAUMATIC EXPERIENCE**: Experiencing a tragic accident, painful medical procedure, or abuse of a sibling, and watching the same, failure or inability to intervene. Circle any that apply to you and list below:

I believe that I experienced the following traumatic experiences:

1._____     7._____

2._____     8._____

3._____     9._____

4._____     10._____

5._____     11._____

6._____     12._____

Some of my negative thoughts and negative feelings resulting from these traumatic experiences are as follows:

NEGATIVE THOUGHTS                 NEGATIVE FEELINGS

1._____     1._____

2._____     2._____

3._____     3._____

4._____     4._____

5._____     5._____

6._____     6._____

Some of the lies I have believed about myself as a result of my traumatic experience(s) are as follows:

1._____     7._____

2._____     8._____

3._____     9._____

4._____     10._____

5._____     11._____

6._____     12._____

Children that grew up with trauma need to be taught the protection and the good, perfect and acceptable will of God for them. (Lamentations 3: 22, 23; Romans 12:1, 2)

Some of the lies I have believed about my Heavenly Father as a result of my traumatic experience(s) are as follows:

1._____     7._____

2._____     8._____

3._____     9._____

4._____     10._____

5._____     11._____

6._____     12._____

**BELIEVING LIES:** Children make things up to fit a child's frame of reference and experience. If children are not taught the truth of who they are in Christ, they are subject to the lies of Satan. Children look up to and respect their parents (God made them that way). Parents that do not own their God given responsibility to teach their children truth and honesty cause them to not know who to trust, to lie themselves, to believe lies, to be confused, to be unable to separate truth from fiction.

Some of the lies that I have believed are as follows:

NEGATIVE THOUGHTS

1._____

2._____

3._____

4._____

5._____

6._____

NEGATIVE FEELINGS

1._____

2._____

3._____

4._____

5._____

6._____

Some of my negative thoughts and negative feelings resulting from believing lies are as follows:

NEGATIVE THOUGHTS

1._____

2._____

3._____

4._____

5._____

6._____

NEGATIVE FEELINGS

1._____

2._____

3._____

4._____

5._____

6._____

Some of the lies I have believed about myself as a result of the lies I was told are as follows:

1._____

2._____

3._____

4._____

5._____

6._____

7._____

8._____

9._____

10._____

11._____

12._____

Children that grow up with lies do not know who or what to believe. They need to be taught that God will guide them into all truth, and that He gives wisdom and discernment to all who ask.

Some of the lies I have believed about my Heavenly Father as a result of the lies I was told are the following:

1._____    7._____
2._____    8._____
3._____    9._____
4._____    10._____
5._____    11._____
6._____    12._____

**UN-CONFESSED SIN(S):** Refusing to ask for forgiveness of sin and turning away. Failure to know the word of God and sin committed unwittingly and/or unknowingly. Some un-confessed sin that you might have experienced in your family are addictions to alcohol, drugs, gambling, work a holism, pre-scription meds, womanizing, affairs, incarceration, etc. (See the list of stage one behaviors, circle and list all that apply.

Some of the un-confessed sins I grew up with are as follows:

1._____    7._____
2._____    8._____
3._____    9._____
4._____    10._____
5._____    11._____
6._____    12._____

Some of my negative thoughts and negative feelings resulting from these un-confessed sins are as follows:

NEGATIVE THOUGHTS                                NEGATIVE FEELINGS

1._____        1._____

2._____        2._____

3._____        3._____

4._____        4._____

5._____        5._____

6._____        6._____

Some of the lies I have believed about myself as a result of the un-confessed sin(s) are as follows:

1._____        7._____

2._____        8._____

3._____        9._____

4._____        10._____

5._____        11._____

6._____        12._____

Children that grow up with caregivers that do not confess their sins believe that there is no consequence to sin. They need to be taught the truth of God's word and His character and to know that all will give an account. (Galatians 6: 7, 8; Proverbs 16:18; Obadiah 3:1; 1 Peter 5:5; Hebrew 3:12, 13).

Some of the lies I have believed about my Heavenly Father as a result of un-confessed sin(s) are as follows:

1._____        7._____

2._____        8._____

3._____        9._____

4._____        10._____

5._____        11._____

6._____        12._____

**UNFORGIVENESS:** Refusing to forgive everyone everything, including God and yourself. This is a form of emotional abuse and teaches a child that God, like their earthly caregiver is unforgiving. Children learn not to forgive themselves or others and grow up with bitterness and many unresolved issues. Without the forgiveness of Christ all are doomed. The adult/child needs to reprogram their mind with the truth of God's word and His forgiving nature and tenderheartedness. (Psalm 130: 1-4; Luke 15: 17-24)

The un-forgiveness I grew up with is as follows:

1._____ 7._____
2._____ 8._____
3._____ 9._____
4._____ 10._____
5._____ 11._____
6._____ 12._____

Some of my negative thoughts and negative feelings resulting from un-forgiveness are as follows:

NEGATIVE THOUGHTS                NEGATIVE FEELINGS

1._____ 1._____
2._____ 2._____
3._____ 3._____
4._____ 4._____
5._____ 5._____
6._____ 6._____

Some of the lies I have believed about myself as a result of un-forgiveness are as follows:

1._____ 7._____
2._____ 8._____
3._____ 9._____
4._____ 10._____
5._____ 11._____
6._____ 12._____

Children that grow up with un-forgiveness learn to carry resentments, un-forgiveness, and bitterness. They teach their children that God is that way also. They teach that it is more important to be right than to keep the peace. These children learn to be stubborn, rigid, bitter and argumentative. Adult/children have to come to understand the truth of God's word and His character and to know that all will give an account.

Some of the lies I have believed about my Heavenly Father as a result of un-forgiveness are as follows:

1._____  7._____
2._____  8._____
3._____  9._____
4._____  10._____
5._____  11._____
6._____  12._____

**DISOBEDIENCE TO GOD'S WORD:** Rebellion against the word of God and failure to know and follow all of the commandments and teachings of the Scriptures sets the child up for failure and an inability to function in a fallen world. They guess at what they are supposed to do. How they should act, think and behave is unknown and un-taught. The only examples for these children are their rebellious parents. They learn to disrespect authority and that the rules do not apply to them. The bible refers to this as a form of witchcraft. Areas of disobedience to the word of God might be idolatry, failure to observe the laws of the land, lack of respect for a particular people group, abuse of people, etc. (See the listing for more examples.) Circle the disobedience you observed in your family and list these areas of rebellion below.

Some of areas of disobedience to the word of God that I grew up with are as follows:

1._____  7._____
2._____  8._____
3._____  9._____
4._____  10._____
5._____  11._____
6._____  12._____

Some of my negative thoughts and negative feelings resulting from disobedience to the word of God are as follows:

NEGATIVE THOUGHTS                    NEGATIVE FEELINGS

1._____    1._____

2._____    2._____

3._____    3._____

4._____    4._____

5._____    5._____

6._____    6._____

Some of the lies I have believed about myself as a result of disobedience to God's word are as follows:

1._____    7._____

2._____    8._____

3._____    9._____

4._____    10._____

5._____    11._____

6._____    12._____

This is also a form of neglect, and emotional abuse. Failure to teach a child that there are consequences to their behavior leads the adult/child to believe that God will not hold them accountable in direct opposition to the teachings of the Scripture. (1 Corinthians 6:9-11).

Some of the lies I have believed about my Heavenly Father as a result of disobedience to God's word are as follows:

1._____    7._____

2._____    8._____

3._____    9._____

4._____    10._____

5._____    11._____

6._____    12._____

**Exercise**: Look at the list(s) above about the negative thoughts and beliefs you have been *reacting* to. Every lie about the character of God is an open door for Satan and his demons to torture you. Every lie that you have believed about who you are is as opportunity and an open door for Satan and his demons. Use the Scriptures below to help you reprogram your mind. Renounce the lies of Satan with the truth of God's word. Scriptures tell us to resist the devil and he will flee.

## THE CHARACTER OF GOD RENOUNCES THE LIES OF SATAN

Adult/children that suffered abuse as children put the face and character of their perpetrator onto God. These lies need to be renounced with the truth of God's word about the character of God. The following Scripture will help to reprogram your mind. Say the Scriptures out loud to yourself. Post the Scriptures on post-it notes of different colors throughout your house. Record the Scriptures using your voice. Speak the Scriptures to yourself. Listen to Christian music that speaks of the true character of God and sing along; in the car, at home, in the shower, and at work if you work at home, or can do so without disturbing others.

*Physical Abuse*

*"The Lord is my rock and my fortress, and my deliverer; my God, my strength, in whom I will trust; my buckler, and the horn of my salvation, and my high tower." Psalm 18:2 KJV*

*"When my father and my mother forsake me, then the Lord will take me up." Psalm 27:10 KJV*

*"Thou art my hiding place; thou shalt preserve me from trouble; thou shalt compass me about with songs of deliverance." Psalm 32:7 KJV*

## Emotional Abuse

*"He kept him as the apple of his eye." Deuteronomy 32:10b KJV*

*"Whoso shall offend one of these little ones which believe in me, it were better for him that a millstone were hanged about his neck, and that he were drowned in the depth of the sea." Matthew 18:6 KJV*

*"So that we may boldly say, The Lord is my helper, and I will not fear what man shall do unto me." Hebrews 13:6 KJV*

## Intellectual Abuse

*"For I know the thoughts that I think towards you, saith the Lord, thoughts of peace, and not of evil, to give you an expected end." Jeremiah 29:11 KJV*

*"Let us therefore come boldly unto the throne of grace, that we may obtain mercy, and find grace to help in time of need." Hebrews 4:16 KJV*

*"For thou will light my candle; the Lord my God will enlighten my darkness." Psalm 18:28 KJV*

*"Do not be conformed any longer to this world, but be transformed by the renewing of your mind." Romans 12:2 KJV*

## Sexual Abuse

*"The Lord hath appeared of old unto me, saying, yea, I have loved thee with an everlasting love; therefore with loving kindness have I drawn thee." Jeremiah 31:3 KJV*

*"He that dwelleth in the secret place of the most High shall abide under the shadow of the Almighty." Psalm 91:1 KJV*

*"He shall cover thee with his feathers, and under his wings shalt thou trust; his truth shall be thy shield and buckler." Psalm 91:4 KJV*

### Neglect

*"Are not two sparrows sold for a farthing? And one of them shall not fall on the ground without your Father. But the very hairs of you head are all numbered. Fear ye not therefore, ye are of more value than many sparrows." Matthew 10:29-31 KJV*

*"He shall feed his flock like a shepherd; he shall gather the lambs with his arms, and carry them in his bosom, and shall gently lead those that are with young." Isaiah 40:11 KJV*

*"The thief cometh not but for to steal, and to kill, and to destroy; I am come that they might have life, and that they might have it more abundantly." John 10:10 KJV*

### Abandonment

*"...And, lo, I am with you alway, even to the end unto the world." Matthew 28:20b KJV*

*"Let your conversation be without covetousness; and be content with such things as ye have; for he hath said, I will never leave thee, nor forsake thee." Hebrews 13:5 KJV*

*"For thus saith the Lord God; Behold, I, even I, will both search my sheep and seek them out. As a shepherd seeketh out his flock in the day that he is among his sheep that are scattered; so will I seek out my*

*sheep, and will deliver them out of all places where they have been scattered in the cloudy and dark day."*
*Ezekiel 34:11, 12 KJV*

### Chronic Long Term Illness

*"Bless the Lord, all my soul, and forget not all his benefits: Who forgiveth all thine iniquities; who healeth all thy diseases; who redeemeth thy life from destruction; who crowneth thee with lovingkindness and tender mercies." Psalm 103:2-4 KJV*

*"But he was wounded for our transgressions, he was bruised for our iniquities; the chastisement of our peace was laid upon him; and with his stripes we are healed." Isaiah 53:5 KJV*

*"And the prayer of faith shall save the sick, and the Lord shall raise him up; and if he hath committed sins, they shall be forgiven him." James 5: 15 KJV*

### Death

*"Yea, though I walk through the valley of the shadow of death, I will fear no evil: for thou art with me: thy rod and thy staff they comfort me." Psalm 23:4 KJV*

*"We are confident, I say, and willing rather to be absent from the body, and to be present with the Lord." 2 Corinthians 5:8 KJV*

*"For me to live is Christ, and to die is gain." Philippians 1:21 KJV*

*"Nothing can separate you from the love of Christ." Romans 8:35 KJV*

### Traumatic Experience

*"It is of the Lord's mercies that we are not consumed, because his compassions fail not. They are new every morning: great is thy faithfulness." Lamentations 3:22, 23 KJV*

*"Cast thy burden upon the Lord and he shall sustain thee: he shall never suffer the righteous to be moved." Psalm 55:22 KJV*

*"The Lord also will be a refuge for the oppressed, a refuge in times of trouble." Psalm 9:9 KJV*

### Believing Lies

*"The lip of truth shall be established for ever; but a lying tongue is but for a moment." Proverbs 12:19 KJV*

*"A false witness shall not be unpunished, and he that speaketh lies shall not escape." Proverbs 19:5 KJV*

*"...When he, the Spirit of truth, is come, he will guide you into all truth." John 16:13a KJV*

*"The Holy Spirit guides you into all truth." John 16:13 KJV*

*Resist the devil. (James 4:7 KJV)*

### Un-confessed Sins

*"If we say that we have no sin, we deceive ourselves, and the truth is not in us. If we confess our sins he is faithful and just to forgive us of our sins and to cleanse us from all unrighteousness." 1 John 1:8, 9 KJV*

*"He healeth the broken in heart, and bindeth up their wounds." Psalm 147:3 KJV*

*"For I will be merciful to their unrighteousness, and their sins and their iniquities will I remember no more." Hebrews 8:12 KJV*

*"And the Lord passed by before him, and proclaimed, the Lord, the Lord God, merciful and gracious, long-suffering, and abundant in goodness and truth, keeping mercy for thousands, forgiving iniquity and transgressions and sin, and that will by no means, clear the guilty; visiting the iniquity of the fathers upon the children, and upon the children's children, unto the third and the fourth generation." Exodus 34:6, 7 KJV*

### Un-forgiveness

*"Then said Jesus, forgive them; for they know not what they do." Luke 23:34a KJV*

*"For if ye forgive men their trespasses, your heavenly Father will also forgive you." Matthew 6:14 KJV*

*"He who conceals his transgression will not prosper, but he who confesses and forsakes them will find compassion." Proverbs 28:13 KJV*

### Disobedience to Gods Word

*"When a man's ways please the Lord, he maketh even his enemies to be at peace with him." Proverbs 16:7 KJV*

*"He who has My commandments and keeps them, it is he who loves Me." John 14:21 NKJV*

*"...Fear not for they that be with us are more than they that be with them." 2 Kings 6:16 KJV*

*"The Lord is not slack concerning his promise, as some men count slackness; but is longsuffering to us-ward, not willing that any should perish, but that all should come to repentance." 2 Peter 3:9 KJV*

*One who grants repentance leading to knowledge of the truth (2 Timothy 2:24-26 KJV)*

*Disclaimer:* In these examples, we ask the Holy Spirit to take you back to the earliest memory of the event that is at the root cause of the pain or problem. We have been asked if these memories are real and questioned about false memory syndrome. These techniques are based on the word of God and sound psychological principles, to be used in a process as a tool, to help individuals heal from problematic lifestyles. They are not designed to be done by unlicensed and/or untrained individuals.

The memory work is not designed to be used in a court of law, nor do we claim its authenticity. A large part of the process is forgiveness work. Ultimately, only the Lord God knows the truth of any given situation. It is only God who can judge the motives of a heart.

When the process is done by untrained professionals, individuals that have taken a course or two and think they know what they are doing, not only can the memory work be false, but the person doing the procedure can cause issues where none existed before including severe harm and even death.

Trained professionals know the difference. They are trained not to ask leading questions or to steer the work in any particular direction. They usually tape the procedure for review at a later date. If the process takes the word of God and helps to set a person free from their bondage, the promise of the Scripture and the gift from Christ to His children has manifested. It is part of the reason that He shed his blood on the cross and bore the stripes on His back so that "you are healed." and "the captives are set free." It is to this end that we write about our experience(s), strength, and hope in applying the Scripture(s). "Take what fits and leave the rest." (12 steps AA, NA, CODA, ACOA, Celebrate Recovery)(Isaiah 53:5, Isaiah 61:1)

*Although Satan is defeated, he still rules this world. His demons tempt, accuse and deceive those that give Satan a foothold, refuse to stand firm in the faith and fail to take their thoughts captive to the obedience of Christ. These are our responsibilities*

192

*"But even unto this day, when Moses is read, the veil is upon their hearts never the less when it shall turn to the Lord, the veil shall be taken away. Now the Lord is that Spirit: and where the Spirit of the Lord is, there is liberty. But we all with open face beholding as in a glass the glory of the Lord, are changed into the same image from glory to glory, even as by the Spirit of the Lord." 2 Corinthians 3:15-18 KJV*

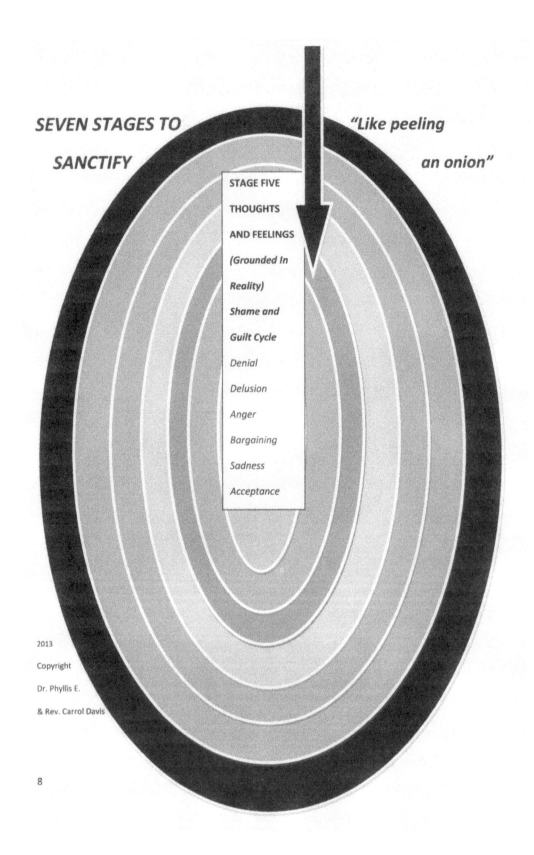

SEVEN STAGES TO
SANCTIFY

"Like peeling
an onion"

STAGE FIVE

THOUGHTS

AND FEELINGS

(Grounded In

Reality)

Shame and

Guilt Cycle

Denial

Delusion

Anger

Bargaining

Sadness

Acceptance

2013
Copyright
Dr. Phyllis E.
& Rev. Carrol Davis

8

# Section 5:

## *Claim Freedom from the Bondage*

# STAGE FIVE: WINNING OVER YOUR PAST: SHAME AND GUILT

*"And hope maketh not ashamed; because the love of God is shed abroad in our hearts by the Holy Ghost which is given unto you." Romans 5:5 KJV*

*"If we confess our sins, He is faithful and just to forgive us our sins and to cleanse us from all unrighteousness." 1 John 1: 9 NKJV*

*T Thoughts and Feelings Grounded In Reality*

*I admit my thoughts and feelings and examine them in the light of God's word.*

*S*hame is about what happened to you and not who you are. (Romans 5:5) *Guilt is about your behavior and what you do.* (1 John 1.9). If you have accepted Christ as your Savior, you are His child, made in His image. You are His perfect creation. He foreknew you in your mother's womb. You are fearfully and wonderfully made. You are His workmanship. If you feel badly about who you are, it is a huge indicator that you are suffering from some form of abuse.

*Guilt is about your behavior and the things you do.* The Holy Spirit guides Christians to repent of bad behavior and cautions you not to do or say anything that is not pleasing to God. Guilt is a good thing that keeps you on the right track. It pricks your conscience and causes you to turn around, change your behavior, repent, and be cleansed.

*Shame on the other hand shuts you down, makes you feel unworthy, and keeps you stuck in dysfunction. It is important to determine the difference between these two principles to recover the person Christ created you to be.*

When you are stuck in shame it is important to get to the exact thoughts that are driving the shameful feeling, so that the lies can be disavowed and replaced with the truth from the word of God. Some of the characteristics of shame are seen in the following stage one issues: addictions, obsessive compulsive disorders, repetition compulsion, re-enactment, self indulging habits, and grandiosity. Some of the defenses of stage two reflecting shame are: power, control, perfectionism, blame, rage, criticism, procrastination, and contempt. Shame is a result of the abuse perpetrated on the now adult-child. When the perpetrator does not own his/or her actions, the child owns the shame as if it were his/or her shame.

The shame based family system can be reflected in rigid roles, and life scripts where the family members are the hero/or heroine, the star, the victim, the problem, the rebel, the little parent, the enabler, the perfect one, the surrogate spouse, the offender, the scapegoat, the lost child and the mascot, and so on.

The family has its own shame based defenses in place to protect the family against discovery. These shame based defenses are: the family spell of delusion: the family member does not remember the trauma, as if it never existed. The family spell of denial: the members of the family deny the problems, even when confronted with overwhelming evidence to the contrary. There are seven rules of a shame based family that can be spoken or covert. These rules help keep the members stuck in shame. Recovery from this programming is to be countered with the truth from the word of God, unhealthy beliefs and lies, dispelled.

***Some rules that will help to identify the "shame based" family and the "counter" to the lies.*** *Circle all the rules that you remember from your childhood and learn to counter your shame based rules with practice, love, compassion and tolerance for that child you once were.*

✓ Always do the right thing. Always be concerned about doing the right thing.

> Counter: The right thing according to whom or what?

✓ If it doesn't go as planned....blame someone.

> Counter: "I accept accountability and responsibility for myself and my behavior." (Accountability and responsibility) "I do not accept (accountability) and (responsibility) for the actions of others, over which I have no control."

✓ Always be in control and do what works: abuse, seduce, plead weakness, change the subject, be controlling and manipulative, run, etc.

> Counter: Identify these tactics and refuse to be manipulated by them.

✓ Absolutely never talk about it. Never talk about your fears. Never talk about the abuse.

> Counter: Break the silence, talk honestly about everything to your accountability person, sponsor, mentor, pastor, and /or counselor.

✓ Absolutely never expect accountability or consistency.

> Counter: Expect accountability and confront inconsistencies.

✓ Stay out of touch with your feelings.

> Counter: Learn to identify all of your feelings and the thoughts driving them.

✓ Deny, deny, deny.

> Counter: Speak the truth of God's word to overpower the darkness with light.


Persons that suffer from the affects of a "shame based" family system carry problems of conversion disorder, disassociation, displacement and idealization issues more commonly than most. At the core of the feelings of the shame based family are issues of hurt, shame and loneliness.


***Guilt offers forgiveness.*** You are taught: *"If we confess our sins, He is faithful and just to forgive us our sins, and to cleanse us from all unrighteousness." 1 John 1:9 KJV*


***Shame keeps you stuck with no way out, until the lies that you believe are exposed.***

God's word speaks of these concepts of *shame* and *guilt*. In Hebrews 12:2 you read about the *shame* of Christ for what was done to Him. He was without sin, guiltless. The sin of the world was heaped on Him: past, present and future. You are the one that deserved to feel the separation from God, not Christ. Yet Christ bore your sins so that you might be saved. Scripture talks about Christ bearing *"OUR SHAME."*

This is a perfect example of how little children feel when they are abused by their parents. They are innocent, undeserving, and yet at a very early age an adult can scar them for life. The child feels shame from the moment the adult abuses and refuses to accept responsibility for their actions. The child carries the shame of the abuser because the abuser refuses to acknowledge their wrong doing. As the years go by, the child represses the memories and learns to be filled with shame. They do not have to do anything wrong to feel these negative emotions, they have carried them all their life.

In the *sanctification* process, the child, now adult learns to disavow the lie about who they are and to claim the truth of the word of God and who God says they are. Many times it takes the acknowledgement and agreement of many other peers to break through the denial. The now adult/child is so rooted in the shame and believes that they deserve to be punished. It is this shameful feeling that can keep an adult from feeling worthy to receive the gift of salvation and the healing of the *sanctification* process.

The cycle of shame and guilt appears just after the discovery of the core issue that has kept you stuck in your pain. It is crucial at this point in the process to push forward through the stages of denial, delusion, bargaining, anger, sadness, and finally acceptance. You sometimes go back and forth through the different stages until you get to acceptance. This is the stage where you truly win over your past and make peace with the negative acting out behaviors. Remember that Christ died for you, carrying your shame and guilt. It was nailed to the tree with Him so that you might live the victorious life He died to give you. Take courage in that and use His strength when yours fails you, push on toward the goal for the prize, your freedom in Christ Jesus.

You can finally have compassion for what you survived. You can forgive yourself and the people that have hurt you, the events or circumstances that caused you grief. It is very important to forgive yourself and God.

As you are making your amends list, remember also to include God. He is a big God. He can handle your anger, sadness, grief and false accusations against Him. He already knows that you have these thoughts and feelings. You are just confessing these thoughts and feelings to your God that has redeemed you, so you can heal. *"Confess your sins to one another so you may heal." James 5:16 KJV Remember* to include yourself on your amends list. God forgives all of your sin and commands you to do the same. Maybe you feel led to make amends to a person that has died. Write an amends letter and read it aloud to your sponsor, counselor, mentor, pastor. Discuss the resentments you have been harboring and pray and ask the Lord Jesus to forgive you for your un-forgiveness, to release you and set you free. Discuss and consider the ways that harboring your resentments and un-forgiveness have affected you in the here and now. How have you cheated yourself out of some of the abundant life Christ died to give you?

**Exercise**

Make a record of these issues below. List the resentment. Name the person that you have held resentment against. Go to the heart of the issue. Remember the pain inflicted, what you thought, how you felt, what you needed and did not get. Tell your perpetrator how that pain has affected you, what it has cost you. Tell them what you think and how you feel about what they did. Discuss them with your accountability partner and/or in small group, with your sponsor, or your pastor. Then forgive them and release them to God's perfect justice. Ask God to forgive you for holding on to your resentments and anger and for letting the sun set on your anger. Use the following steps to help you stay on track.

1. Name the resentment and who you hold resentments toward.
2. Talk about how their actions affected you.
3. Tell them what you think about what they did. Counter any lies you believe as a result of their behavior and the event for which you are holding resentments.
4. Tell them how you feel about what they did: Angry, sad, hurt, fearful, etc.
5. Tell them the other people that were harmed as a result of what they did.

6. Tell them that what they did was abusive. That there is no legitimate excuse for their behavior.

7. Tell them you release them to God's perfect justice because you are commanded to in obedience to Christ.

8. Tell God you are angry at Him for allowing it to happen. (You just own the feelings that are there. God already knows what you think and how you feel.)

9. Ask God to forgive you for your un-forgiveness, for letting the sun set on your anger, for not following His word.

10. Command the demons of un-forgiveness, anger, sadness, and fear to leave. They have no authority to be in your life. You have forgiven the person and their actions. You no longer hold them accountable. They owe you nothing. You released them to God's perfect justice.

11. You have asked God to forgive you for your un-forgiveness and you let God know you forgive Him although He did nothing wrong, you had a false belief that he did. Correct the lies and false beliefs about God with the truth about His character from the word of God.

12. Make sure that you forgive from the heart of the matter where the pain is. Otherwise the forgiveness work will not be complete and you will still be in bondage. If you have no emotional release you are not in the heart of the matter.

    List all of the steps below to make certain you covered each one.

_____

_____

_____

_____

_____

_____

_____

_____

_____

_____

_____

_____

_____

_____

_____

_____

_____

After you have thoroughly processed a memory, you may want to go to persons you have harmed to make amends. You may want to make right a situation where you have harmed someone else. *Do so only with caution*, the advice of wise counsel and the support of friends in an accountability group or with a therapist, and or your pastor. Many people are not safe and such confessions could do further harm, make the situation worse, or harm someone else. Pray and ask God to show you to whom or what you need to make amends and then do so with support and prayerfully, if God so leads. Scripture cautions us not to throw our pearls to the swine for a reason; they may turn and rend you to pieces. *"Give not that which is holy unto the dogs, neither cast ye your pearls before swine, lest they trample them under their feet, and turn again and rend you." Matthew 7:6 "Reprove not a scorner, lest he hate thee: rebuke a wise man, and he will love thee." Proverbs 9:8.* This is a discernment issue and needs wise counsel.

Many times the amends you make are living amends to God to live your life in a Godly way while encouraging others to do the same by your example, exhortation, and teaching.

*"Therefore since we have this ministry, as we received mercy, we do not lose heart, but we have renounced things hidden because of shame, not walking in craftiness or adulterating the word of God, but by their manifestation of truth." 2 Corinthians 4: 1, 2*

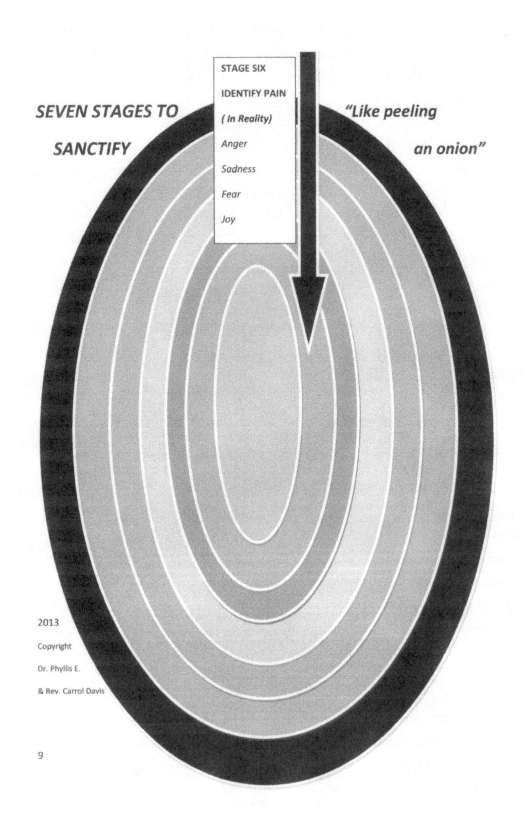

SEVEN STAGES TO

SANCTIFY

"Like peeling

an onion"

STAGE SIX

IDENTIFY PAIN

( In Reality)

Anger

Sadness

Fear

Joy

2013

Copyright

Dr. Phyllis E.

& Rev. Carrol Davis

9

# Section 6:

## *He Turns Your Scars to Stars.*

# STAGE SIX: UNDERSTANDING YOUR PAIN

*"Keep and guard your heart with all vigilance and above all that you guard,*
*for out of it flow the springs of life." Proverbs 4:23 AMP*

*I Identify Pain: The Grieving Process*

*I admit my pain and accept healing by grieving my losses.*

This stage of the process feelings tumble out in what seems like a never ending process. The tears flow like a river. The anger feels terrifying and destructive. The fear shakes the body in what appears to be a convulsive state. Although this state can be unnerving, if one understands what is going on, it is less terrifying. These are the feelings that have been bottled up for all of these years. It is this repression that has stopped the emotional and sometimes intellectual development of the person beyond the years of the trauma. For example, if someone starts to use alcohol and drugs at the age of sixteen, their emotional development might reflect the responses and approach to life that a sixteen year old would have even though they are fifty biological years of age. If an adult were traumatized at the age of two or three and the issues have been unresolved, they might respond to any conflict the way a two or three year old child would. You might hear a fifty year old man claim in agonizing grief, "I thought they were my friend. They said they don't want to be my friend anymore." The grammar, sentence content, sentence structure, and tonality might sound just like a two year old is talking.

Elizabeth Kubler Ross in her work on "Death and Dying" talks about the stages of the grieving process when one is processing a death. I believe that a much similar process transpires as someone processes the core issues of their life. There is a death, parse of the facts as they once knew them.

**Example**

For example, an adult/child discovers that the "Leave it to Beaver" family they grew up in is a fantasy. The family that they grew up in was really dysfunctional and abusive. It can be a real shock. Everything that one believes or has believed becomes questionable. Ones' reality is shaken to the core causing you to go through a process similar to the one described by Ross in "Death and Dying; what Ross calls the grieving process. Although there is not a death, there is a loss, i.e. your reality is shaken, a death of the lies and beliefs of childhood.

**Exercise Grieving**

The levels listed below are the different levels you must experience in order to move through the grieving process. Study the different levels and try to determine which level you are on in accepting the truth of your life. Circle where you think you are in the grieving process. Discuss and receive feedback from your accountability partner and or your small group. Record you feelings at the end of the exercise.

*Delusion*: There is no conscious awareness of the event. The memory is repressed.

*Denial:* Its' not true...I made it up. There is a refusal to admit the truth despite overwhelming evidence to the contrary.

*Bargaining*: Well, it might be true; but I deserved it. Or, it would not have happened if _____. I am to blame. I must have done something wrong that justifies the behavior.

*Anger:* The anger is usually side-ways anger, directed at the pastor, dialogue partner, God, process group, or self instead of the perpetrator.

*Sadness:* The grief is overwhelming sadness, fear and anger cycling back and forth.

*Acceptance:* It must be true. It makes sense. This is why I have done....thought....reacted in such unhealthy ways. The feelings that were bigger than the event now make sense in light of this new information.

**Prayer**

*Heavenly Father, Holy Spirit, give me your wisdom and discernment as I continue on this journey of discovery. Give me your strength for the journey. Father, give me the courage to face the truth of my past. Where I have deceived myself, I ask for your forgiveness. Where I have unwittingly deceived others, forgive me. Cleanse me with your truth and set me free from my deception(s) and the tools Satan and his army of demons have used to steal my joy. Set me free to live the abundant life Christ died to give me and to experience the joy of my salvation. Amen*

**Exercise**

Break up into your groups. Give each person a chance to talk about what they have discovered. As they tell you about what they have discovered, notice what level of the grieving process they are on. At the conclusion of their process work, let each group member give feed back to the "truth teller." Continue around the circle until each person has processed their issue(s) and has had a turn to tell their "truth," the story of their discovery.

Use the space below to record the level of grieving for each group member. Start with yourself.

*Member    Member's Discovery  Level on the Grieving Process*

_____    _____    _____

_____    _____    _____

_____    _____    _____

_____    _____    _____

_____    _____    _____

Notice how you felt giving feedback to your group members. Were you reluctant to be honest, fearful you would hurt someone's feelings? Is it hard for you to be honest with others, even when it is for their good? Was it easy to give feedback to others? Was it hard to receive feedback from others? Healthy people see their life as a work in process, a daily "picking up their cross" for the cause of Christ.

A person does not always go through these stages in order, nor does a person complete the process without sometimes going back and forth between stages. Be patient and encouraging with yourself and others. People work through these stages at varying degrees of time. The important thing is the process.

This flood of emotions can be like a dam breaking. You will experience feelings, some of which you have never experienced before. God designed you to have all of your emotions. They can serve as a guide to let you know when you are hurt, in pain, need attention both physically and emotionally. Your anger helps serve as a guide that you need to set boundaries and can prevent you from being harmed.

**Exercise**

Access to all of your emotions allows you to be the person God created you to be. You tend to label them positive or negative, yet all emotions are good for you and serve a purpose. God made you that way. Below is a list of emotions. Opposite each emotion that you would tend to label negative is the emotion that you tend to label positive. Circle any emotion below that you are not comfortable expressing. Practice expressing the emotions you have repressed by telling the group an experience using the emotion you are not comfortable with. Next allow the group to give you feed back. Were you congruent? If you said you were angry, did your face agree? If not, if you said one thing and your face and body language said another make a note of the difference below.

The Issue: Emotional

| Event/Person | Expression Intended | My Words Said | My Face & Body Said |
| --- | --- | --- | --- |
|  |  |  |  |
|  |  |  |  |
|  |  |  |  |
|  |  |  |  |
|  |  |  |  |
|  |  |  |  |
|  |  |  |  |
|  |  |  |  |
|  |  |  |  |
|  |  |  |  |

## EMOTIONS:

**NEGATIVE**

- Angry
- Sad
- Fearful

**POSITIVE**

Happy

Joyful

Peaceful

Most likely, the emotions that you label negative are labeled such, because you were not allowed to feel those emotions as a child and are not comfortable with them. As you grow in Christ and the *sanctification* process, you will learn to express all of your emotions in a way that honors Christ and works to your good and His glory.

In the beginning stages of the *sanctification* process and discovery you limit your reference to the feelings of anger, sadness, fear and joy. Most all of your emotions are an expression of one of these emotions. The first goal is to learn the difference between a thought and a feeling. Limiting the reference of feelings to one of the above makes your task easier. As you grow in Christ and your ability to sort through the differences in thoughts and feelings, you become more equipped to express your emotions in varying degrees. You also learn to use your feelings as indicators of where your life is out of balance and what you need.

**Exercise Working a Program of Continued Sanctification**

Spending time alone with Christ in prayer and meditation speeds the journey. Scripture teaches you that the Lord will be your teacher. Earthly teachers, mentors, books, prayer warriors, pastors, sponsors all help you on your journey. The ultimate authority is always the word of God. If any teaching varies or discounts the word of God, the teaching is false and you are to look to the Bible as the correct counsel.

Set aside thirty minutes a day to start. If you are a morning person, set aside the time in the morning. If you are an evening person, make your time in the evening. Read something from the Bible every day. Start with a realistic goal, a chapter or two a day. Read something from Christian literature on the area of *sanctification* you are submitting to Christ for transformation.

In the beginning of your process, go to a meeting with like minded individuals committed to the process of *sanctification*. We recommend ninety meetings in ninety days. Choose groups that are dealing with similar issues, if possible. Attendance at church, prayer meetings, bible study, recovery groups, therapy groups, and small groups all count toward the ninety meeting requirements.

Pray and ask God into your life every morning. Talk to him about your needs, wants and challenges. Listen for answer to prayer, listen for guidance. God answers through the word of God, the bible, accountability people, sponsors, recovery literature. Practice listening and checking out what you hear with your sponsor, small group, or accountability partner. Get on your knees every evening and thank God for your day, for His provision and for keeping you safe.

Continue to record your progress in your workbook and or in a journal.

Trust your Spirit as you are taught Scripture and the proper application. If you have a check in your spirit about something that you have been taught, pray for understanding. It is the Holy Spirit's job to warn you against false teaching and misapplication of the word of God. Many well meaning and misinformed people can lead you astray. Always seek wise counsel. *"Where no counsel is, the people fall: but in the multitude of counselors there is safety." Proverbs 11:14 KJV* and *"Trust in the Lord with all thine heart; and lean not unto thine own understanding. In all thy ways acknowledge Him and He shall direct thy paths." Proverbs 3:5, 6* Learning to rightly apply the word of God to your life, problems and the decisions you must make is a life long process. You must have an intimate relationship with your Savior and listen as He speaks to you, guides you. It is the Holy Spirit's job to interpret Scripture and when you pray and ask for clarity, your prayers will be answered. You must know the entire content of the word of God to rightly apply the word and to discern accurately. Remember also that God judges the motives of your heart and will know when you are doing your best to grow in maturity in Him.

Remember that you have issues, you are on your own individual journey and many people provide inaccurate information through the filters of their own dysfunctional history. Ultimately you are all accountable to your Heavenly Father for the gifts, talents and abilities that He has given you. It will be before Him alone that you will stand to give an account of all you say and do. We personally have plenty to do, to do all that we see our Father doing without insisting that others do it "our way."

## Prayer

*God, grant me the serenity*

*to accept the things I can not change,*

*the courage to change the things I can,*

*and the wisdom to know the difference.*

*Living one day at a time,*

*Enjoying one moment at a time;*

*accepting hardship as a pathway to peace;*

*taking as Jesus did, this sinful world as it is;*

*not as I would have it;*

*Trusting that You will make all things right*

*if I surrender to Your will;*

*so that I may be reasonably happy in this life*

*and supremely happy with You forever in the next.*

*AMEN*

(The Serenity Prayer by

Reinhold Niebuhr)

*"If the Son therefore shall make you free, ye shall ne free indeed." John 8:36*

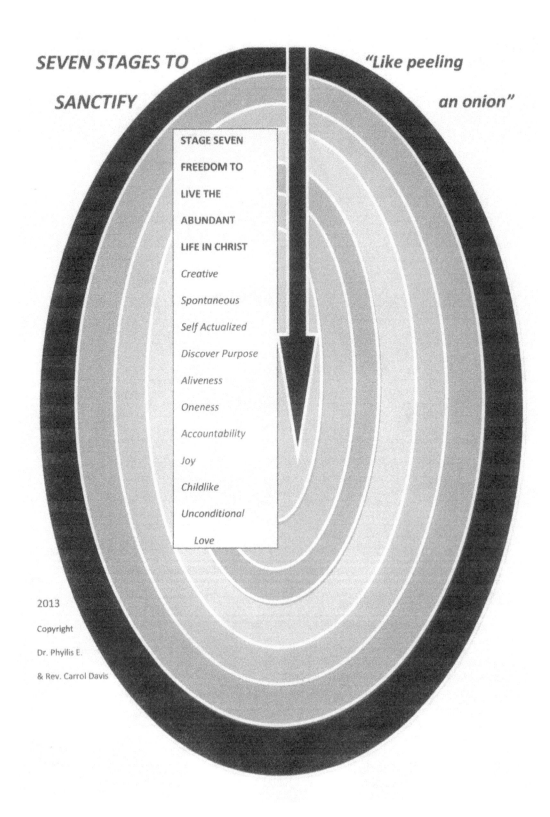

SEVEN STAGES TO SANCTIFY

"Like peeling an onion"

STAGE SEVEN

FREEDOM TO

LIVE THE

ABUNDANT

LIFE IN CHRIST

*Creative*

*Spontaneous*

*Self Actualized*

*Discover Purpose*

*Aliveness*

*Oneness*

*Accountability*

*Joy*

*Childlike*

*Unconditional*

*Love*

2013

Copyright

Dr. Phyllis E.

& Rev. Carrol Davis

# Section 7:

## *He Sets the Captives Free;*
## *Becoming the Person Christ Meant for You to Be*

# STAGE SEVEN: LIVING THE VICTORIOUS LIFE CHRIST DIED TO GIVE YOU

*"For I know the plans I have for you, saith the Lord, plans not to harm you,*

*but to give you a hope and a future." Jeremiah 29:11 KJV*

*"Let this mind be in you which was also in Christ Jesus." Philippians 2:5 KJV*

**F** *Freedom to Live the Abundant Life: I accept my freedom as a gift from God.*

As you emerge from the bondage of your past, the person Christ created you to become emerges. Characteristics that were not readily apparent are visible. You become more joyful, creative, playful, and resourceful. You continue to deepen in your relationship with Christ. You are more honest, open, and willing to explore areas in your life that are not fully *sanctified.* As the apostle Paul states, *"They keep their eyes on the prize,"* as God transforms them into the creatures He created them to become from *"glory to glory."* (Philippians 3:14, 2 Corinthians 3:18)

God transforms and empowers you to become more and more like Him. You learn to be responsible to others, not responsible for them. You learn to view and love others as Christ taught you by His example.

You learn to show empathy by encouraging, sharing, confronting, and being honest, leveling with others, sensitive with a listening ear. You show concern for others when you relate person to person, expressing your thoughts and feelings, sharing your experience(s), strength, and hope. You learn that you are helpers and guides, yet you do not do for others what they can and should do for themselves. You expect responsibility from others, you trust and let go, and let God. God is a gentleman. He never barges into an area of someone's life that is not submitted to Him. In your process of transformation you learn to model Christ's behavior more and more as you understand how to apply the principles that He taught you in His word. You empower people, you no longer enable them. Jesus did not; why should you?

### *You Learn that Control is an Illusion*

Enabling is doing for someone else what they should, and could do for themselves. It is being responsible for the actions of others, over which you have no control, and even Christ does not hold you accountable. Some characteristics of enabling behaviors were listed before. In this last stage you have learned not to fall for the manipulations. Some of the characteristics which you have now mastered are as follows. Circle all that you have mastered. I no longer:

- ✓ Accept lies for the truth, being misled or outsmarted
- ✓ Allow exploitation, or manipulating
- ✓ Cover up the truth, losing my temper
- ✓ Preach and lecture or withdraw
- ✓ Argue or threaten
- ✓ Nag or postpone plans
- ✓ Make excuses for others to schools, employers, etc.
- ✓ Participate in unhealthy behavior: drinking, drugging, abusing, etc.
- ✓ Destroy the property of others; drugs, and alcohol, etc.

Christ allows you to freely choose to follow Him, to accept Him and His ways. As painful as it was for Him, He allowed the rich young ruler to walk away when he refused to follow all of God's commands. (Matthew 19:21) You have to do the same. Control is an illusion. You cannot control yourselves, sometimes, much less others.

Channels of communication and learning were discussed earlier. The facts and research have shown that people process information in several *channels of communication*: *what you see, what you hear, what you feel, smell, and taste*. As you process the real issues, you receive the gifts of healing that Christ died to give you and the channels that were shut down begin to heal. An example of this type of healing occurred with a man you will call Jerry.

**Example: Healing of Vision**

Jerry wore "coke bottle" glasses. His prescription was so strong that the lenses looked like coke bottles. During his *sanctification* process; the doctor changed the Rx for his glasses on numerous occasions. Each time the lenses were changed to a weaker prescription. It seems that there were several incidents in Jerry's childhood that were too painful for him to *"see."* Jerry repressed the vivid images of the trauma deep into the recesses of his mind. God in his sovereignty allowed Jerry to temporarily forget the painful memories until it was safe to remember. As Jerry explored his acting out behavior, lack of friendships and problems in relationships, he uncovered the memories too painful to *"see"* before. Jerry completed this part of his journey with the tossing of the glasses. He no longer required the thick, "coke bottled lens" glasses to see, as he remembered, processed and forgave, he only required glasses for reading. The visual channel that had been shut down was open once again.

*Values Change. Discerning Differences of Wants and Needs*

The acid raindrops of life, the besetting sins of self and others poured into a child at an early age cause the adult-child to be unable to separate who they are from what they do. They also have trouble separating

215

what they need from what they want. In the process of *sanctification* the individual learns to distinguish the difference between who they are and what they do. Values change, hearts change as God transforms a life. You learn that Christ meets your needs always. In His love and mercy, He refuses wants that are not within His will and/or might harm you.

Scripture teaches you that you are not your behaviors. Christ loves His children, He hates their sins. Christ never abandons His child, yet God is too pure and holy to look on sin. You are not your sin. You are children of God saved by His grace. Although God hates sin, you are redeemed, your sins forgiven and He remembers them no more, *"for I will forgive their iniquity, and I will remember their sin no more."* *Jeremiah 31:34.*

Christ promises to take care of His children, to provide for them food, shelter, clothing and all of their needs. He does not promise steak dinners, designer clothes and a sports car in the driveway. In the process of becoming, you learn the difference between a need and a want. The abundant life of Christ's promises gives you the peace that only God can give. Whether wealthy or poor in material possessions, you are rich in the abundance of the things of Christ. He takes your heart of stone and transforms it into a heart of flesh. You experience contentment in your life regardless of the surrounding circumstances. You know that everything that happens to you is sifted through the loving hands of your Savior. You understand that being a Christian, submitted to the *sanctification* of your Savior does not mean "smooth sailing." Life in a fallen world brings opposition and storms to the life of the *"sanctified"* and the unsaved. The difference is the confidence to weather the storm and the knowledge of who is in control. You get out of the driver's seat and allow God to direct you. As you mature you look at challenges as opportunities for God to grow you. You have more peace, even in the midst of the storm. You rely on the promises of God. Your faith grows as you experience the true character of God, His love and provision for you.

The beliefs and values of your past are examined in the light of the truth of God's word and Satan's lies. You learn to discount the lies and cling to the truth. Your brain is like a computer…garbage in…garbage out. If you are programmed by your care givers that *"no matter what you do, it is never enough."* and you believe this message, you are living your life based on the lies of Satan. *Sanctification* teaches you to *take your thoughts captive to the obedience of Christ. (2 Corinthians 10:5)* You learn to replace your negative thoughts and lies with the word of God. Instead of being driven by the words, *"no matter what I do it is never enough,"* you hear the Lord's words: *"Well done thou good and faithful servant."* Matthew 25:21 This is just one example of the transformation process of *sanctification* as it relates to false values and beliefs. There are thousands of other examples. As you travel through this part of the journey you will discover the specific false belief(s) and lies that have driven your acting out behavior.

**Exercise: Countering Satan's Lies with God's Truth**

List some of the lies that drove your thoughts and actions below. Next write the truth from God's word that you used to counter the lie.

Satan's Lies                                    God's truths from His word

_____          _____

_____          _____

_____          _____

_____          _____

_____          _____

**Prayer**

*Affirm: By the power of the blood of Jesus, I take my thoughts captive to the obedience of Christ. I denounce the lie(s) of Satan* _____. *I affirm the truth of the word of God about me, my life and the character of Jesus Christ, my Savior, my deliverer,* _____

_____   _____

_____

*In Jesus Mighty Name, Amen*

Repeat the affirmations of God's word and denounce the lies of Satan for every lie you have believed. Close the door to Satan and his demonic influence in your life.

### *Mutual Interdependency and Healthy Relationships*

The goal set by Christ to become equally yoked in marriage becomes more attainable between two people that make Christ the head of their home, each person striving to become all Christ created him / her to be. Mutual dependency of unhealthy relationships is transformed into healthy interdependence. Two people choose to live together and explore their process as individuals, and as a unit, a couple.

They do not see each other through the lens of delusion. They acknowledge each others' faults, hurts, hang-ups, and assist each other in the *sanctification* process. Disagreements become opportunities to explore areas of bondage and the opportunity to be set free. Conflicts and challenges draw the couple closer to God in prayer. Christ is the glue that keeps the marriage of two very different and separate people with different likes and dislikes, together and focused on common interests and goals.

### Exercise: Pray To God Individually. Pray to God As A Couple.

Take turns praying for your relationship, your needs, your problems, your challenges. Pray for guidance, direction. Ask for forgiveness of sins. Pray for your friends and their needs. Pray for your enemies. Pray for God to bless them. Pray breath prayers, from your heart in your own words. Pray for God to reveal things to you, you do not know.

### *Communication Skills Improve and the Ability to Set Boundaries*

Communication skills improve as the individuals learn to accept responsibility and accountability for their part in the relationship. Use of what therapists label "4 part I statements" as a healthy way to communicate and negotiate differences, becomes routine instead of awkward and cumbersome.

The use of "4 part I statements" causes one to own their thoughts and feelings and communicate clearly what they need and want. This exercise prevents many dysfunctional conversations and teaches you to listen to others.

**Prayer**

*Heavenly Father I commit my plans to you, leaning not on my own understanding but in all my ways I ask you to direct my paths. Help me to follow all of your commands and let my life be a pleasing sacrifice to you in all I say and do. Guide this process; show me the way, your perfect way, not the permissive way, but rather the exact path that you laid out for me before time began.*

*Lead me to wisdom, discernment, and wise counsel. Teach me to do all that I see you doing that I might be a doer of the word and not a hearer only. I pray for the healing that your Son died to give me. Let my life be filled with the abundant blessings of the promise and a reflection of all that you died to give me. It is in Jesus sweet name, the name above all names that I pray.*
*Amen*

**Exercise**

<u>4 Part I Statements:</u>
"Person A" expresses a feeling about an event and what they thought about the event. Person "A" expresses a need or want and sets a boundary (that is within their control):

I feel _____ when I _____ I think _____. I need/want _____; if you can not help me get my needs met, I choose to _____. (Boundary)

**Active Listening**:

"Person B" repeats identically what he/she heard.

I heard you say that you feel _____when you _____.
You think _____. What you need or want is _____. If I can not
help you get your needs met, you choose to _____. (Boundary)

In the above example, the person A is communicating by expresses his/her feelings, the event causing
the feelings, the thoughts about the event, and asks for what they need or want. The addition of a boundary
is sometimes necessary. This addition expresses a limit if the person does not receive what they have asked
for. The boundary must be in the person's control and they must be able to carry it out. An idle threat is
not a boundary.

You have a right to get your needs met, you do not have a right to determine the source. God is your
provider and He determines the source to meet your needs.

Two people can see the same event and come away with totally different thoughts and feelings about
the event. You come from different backgrounds, experiences, cultures, geographic regions and conse-
quently you process information through these different filters. Communication skills can help to eliminate problems and areas of misunderstanding.

**Exercise "4 Part I Statements"**
*Break up into groups of two, and take turns using the "4 Part I Statements"*

Person A uses the model to express a feeling and a thought about an event while asking for what they
need or want, while setting a boundary. Person B sits in a chair facing Person A. Persons A and Person B
maintains eye contact and listens intently during the exercise. Person B repeats back to Person A what he/
she believes was said, verbatim. Person A confirms that "Yes that is what I said" or "No. that is not what I

said." If Person B did not repeat what Person A said exactly, Person A repeats the "4 part I statement" and gives Person B another chance to repeat what was said.

Then switch roles. Person B expresses a feeling and a thought about an event while asking for what they need or want and sets a boundary. Person A actively listens and repeats the exact words of Person B. If Person A does not repeat the exact words, Person B should repeat his/her "4 part I statement" and give Person A the second chance to repeat the exact words.

This takes practice. It does not come automatically. People struggle with expressing their needs and wants. People struggle to find a boundary that is within their control and is enforceable. Active listening can be a challenge. It is a challenge for people to learn to separate their thoughts from their feelings. Many people don't even know what they need or want. Some are afraid to ask for what they want. This is a learning tool to help improve communication skills.

Have fun, enjoy the process and learn a new skill that just might come in handy in times of crisis. Learn now while there is no threat and you can enjoy the process. Pick something to work on that is not threatening. Wait until you have more skill to move into an area that might "ruffle the feathers."

A good example of the use of a "4 part I statement" follows: A Christian woman is in a relationship where she is exposed to constant verbal and emotional abuse by her husband. She is tired and exhausted from dealing with the abuse, yet she loves her husband and does not want to leave him. She can stop the escalation of the violence by employing the "4 part I statement" as follows:

❖ I feel *angry* when I *hear* yelling and cursing. I *think* I am in danger and I do not hear what is being said. I *need* a lower tone and volume to hear what is being said. If you choose to ignore my wishes, I will leave the room, the next time I hear yelling and cursing. (Notice that the boundary is within her control and does not need the cooperation of the spouse to be enforced).

*"4 Part I Statements" are only a tool. They assume good will between the partners. If real danger is present, abuse continues, and or escalates, emergency measures are necessary.*

*Have money, identification, medication, credit cards, important papers, toiletries and clothes packed in a bag, stored outside the home for you to collect at a moments notice. Have contact numbers of doctors, support persons and a place to stay in an emergency in the bag as well as an extra set of keys. It is not to your good or God's glory for you to suffer abuse.*

As couples engage in their own *sanctification* process, the journey together is easier. Practicing healthy communication skills becomes easier. Knowing each others' buttons, triggers and history makes keeping the peace much easier. You can even be accountability partners as your spouse struggles with issues and character defects that Christ is transforming in their life. You all need accountability partners outside of the relationship to help you stay accountable. Scriptures talk about your relationships and accountability to each other: *Lamentations 3:40 KJV: "Let us examine our ways and test them, and let us return to the Lord.,* and James *5:16 KJV: "Therefore confess your sins to each other and pray for each other so that you may be healed."* and *Galatians 6:1 KJV: "Brothers, if someone is caught in a sin, you who are spiritual should restore him gently. But watch yourself, or you also may be tempted."* Scripture refers to being accountable to one another, *Proverbs 27:17: "Iron sharpened iron; so a man sharpened the countenance of his friend."*

### Ability to Take Your Thoughts Captive: Recognize Attacks of the Enemy

Abuse and trauma cause a symptom referred to by psychologists and doctors as dissociation. We believe this condition is a gift from God that allows children to survive some of the horrors that they were exposed to. The type of abuse and its severity, the duration of each abusive episode, and the extent of the abuse over time determine the amount of dissociation connected to a repressed memory, as well as the extent of the amnesic barriers. This dissociation can manifest itself in many different forms, from highway hypnosis, which you are all familiar with, to multiple ego states. A good example would be highway hypnosis. It is the state you are in when driving for long distances, as if in a fog, and suddenly you notice that you have missed your exit.

The Bible talks about this phenomenon when the Scriptures teach that to be absent from the body is to be present with the Lord. *(2 Corinthians 5:8)*. Numerous stories of death, dying and returning to life talk of this phenomenon. Many talk about the long silver cord that connects the body and soul. We believe that God in His infinite wisdom designed your body to survive the sins of this world. Even in the midst of extreme abuse and the remembering of the same, people give accounts of Christ's being there with them in the "fire," just like Shadrach, Meshach and Abednego. (Daniel 3:5) *Sanctification* erases the dissociative barriers and releases memories in order to process: to release the repressed emotions, feelings, sounds, sights, and thoughts; to replace those negative thoughts and beliefs with the truth of God.

It becomes easier to *"take our thoughts captive to the obedience of Christ"* as you continue to practice. It becomes easier to recognize the enemy, his tactics, and to dispel the lies and beliefs he has implanted in your heart. Christ takes your heart of stone and changes it to a heart of flesh. (2 Corinthians 10:5, Ezekiel 36:26 KJV)

**Exercise: Recognize the Attacks of the Enemy**

List the ways that Satan tries to attack you. List the ways that Satan tries to attack your spouse. What are the lies he tells you? What are the lies he tells your spouse? Counter with the truth from the word of God.

Satan's Lies to Me             Counter With God's Truth

_____     _____

_____     _____

_____     _____

Satan's Lies to My Spouse         Counter With God's Truth

_____     _____

_____     _____

_____     _____

What Do You Suppose Satan's Motives Are? How Does He Steal From You? How Does He Kill You? How Does He Destroy You? Knowing Specifically How He Attacks You Will Put You On The Alert For His Attacks.

_____

_____

_____

_____


An example would be that he steals from you by taking your joy, getting you angry at each other instead of the enemy. Remember your battle is not against "flesh and blood" but against "principalities, powers, rulers of the darkness of this world, spiritual wickedness in high places."(Ephesians 6:12 KJV)


### Order and Balance Replace Chaos and Confusion


Your life becomes more ordered and more balanced. Work, play, love, relationships, and spiritual growth are more balanced. Your life is no longer thrown off track with dysfunction at the center of your life. When the God of order is in the center of all you say and do, your life reflects His order. You are able to set appropriate priorities…to say "yes" when you mean "yes," and "no," when you mean "no." You are less driven by fear, guilt and the expectations of others as you look to God to direct you daily. Chaos and confusion, the curses of Satan, are replaced by the gifts of God sent to you through His Son Jesus, "…*peace I leave with you…." John 14:27*

What you say, think and feel become more congruent with your actions in all areas of your life. You learn that your communication with others is not only verbal, but also non-verbal. Your actions, touch, and expressions talk just as loudly as your words, and you strive for congruency in all you communicate. You learn to drop the defenses of the past and to communicate openly and honestly with others about what you are thinking and how you are feeling. You learn to recognize when your feelings are "bigger than the event," your history is being triggered, and you are reacting to the past rather than responding to the present. You take responsibility for your feelings and submit your overreactions to Christ and the *sanctification* process.

### You Become More Responsible and Accountable

You learn to own your feelings and to take responsibility for your actions, good and bad, and to make amends when your behavior has hurt or harmed someone else. You start to act out the Scriptures in your daily life and to follow the dictates of the word. When you know someone has something against you, you go to them and try to make things right. (Matthew 5:23, 24)

When you see your brother caught in a sin, you are to go to him/her and try to restore according to the dictates of Galatians 6:1. You strive to be a doer of the word, not a hearer only. You continue to use the model when you are stuck or acting out to get to the core issues, resolve the issues, overcome the feelings, and get back on track.

Continued growth in Christ delivers the promises of the abundant life as you grow to be more and more like Him. Your dysfunction and character defects are replaced by the fruits of the spirit: love, joy, peace, patience, kindness, goodness, faith, gentleness, and self control. (Galatians 5:22, 23)

### You Recognize Yourself and Others as A Work in Process: Progress Not Perfection

You learn to acknowledge your character defects and those of others as a work in progress, "progress, not perfection" as you allow the *"...author and finisher of our faith"* to continue to *sanctify* you from *"glory to glory."* (Hebrews 12: 2, 2 Corinthians 3:18)

At this point in the process, one is usually well on their way to discovering what direction their life should take, and to know to what purpose God has called them. Your *sanctification* process becomes your story and your testimony. *"They overcame him by the blood of the Lamb and the word of their testimonies and loved not their lives unto death." Revelation 12:11 KJV*

Most often the scars of the past become the road map to the future. Your sovereign Lord does not waste anything. He even holds your tears in a bottle in heaven. God uses His *"cracked pots and broken vessels"* to tell his story. He turns scars to stars. The pain in your life is a key to your mission. Discover your story and learn how to tell it for your good and His glory.

There is oneness at this stage in the areas of your life that you have allowed the Holy Spirit to *"sanctify,"* *"That they may all be one: as thou, Father, are in me, and I in thee, that they also may be one in you: that the world may believe that thou hast sent me." John 17:21 KJV*

**Exercise: He Turns Your Scars to Stars**

***The promises of the Scripture come alive as you experience more of the abundant life Christ died to give you.*** *Circle the ways that God has transformed your pain for your good and His glory.*

❖ 1. Creative: John 14:26 AMP

*"But the comforter, which is the Holy Ghost, whom the Father will send in my name, He shall teach you all things, and bring to your remembrance, whatsoever I have said unto you."*

❖ 2. Spontaneous: Philippians 2:5 KJV

*"Let the mind be in you which was also in Christ Jesus."*

❖ 3. Self Actualized: Jeremiah 29:11 KJV

*"For I know the thoughts and plans that I have for you, says the Lord, thoughts and plans for welfare and peace and not for evil."*

❖ 4. Life Purpose Discovered: Jeremiah 29:11 NKJV

*"For I know the thoughts that I think toward you, says the Lord, thoughts of peace and not of evil to give you a future and a hope."*

❖ 5. Aliveness: Matthew 10:39 KJV, and John 11:25-26 KJV

*"He that findth his life shall loose it: and he that looseth his life for my sake shall find it."*

*"I am the resurrection and the life, He who believes in me, though he may die, he shall live, and whoever lives and believes in me shall never die. Do you believe this?"*

❖ 6. Oneness: John 17:21 KJV

*"That they may all be one: as thou, Father, are in me, and I in thee, that they also may be one in you: that the world may believe that thou hast sent me."*

❖ 7. Accountability: James 5:16 KJV

*"Confess your faults one to another and pray one for another, that ye may be healed."*

❖ 8. Joy: Psalms 51:12 KJV

*"Restore unto me the joy of thy salvation."*

❖ 9. Unconditional Love: John 13:35 KJV

*"By this shall all men know that you are my disciples; that you have love one to another."*

❖ 10. Childlike (not Childish): Matthew 18:3 NKJV

*"...assuredly I say to you, unless you are converted and become as little children, you will by no means enter the kingdom of heaven."*


*"For I know the thoughts that I think toward you, saith the Lord, thoughts of peace and not of evil, to give you an expected end. Then shall ye call upon me, and ye shall go and pray unto me, and I will hearken unto you. And ye shall seek me, and find me when ye shall search for me with all your heart. and I will be found of you, saith the Lord; and I will turn away your captivity and I will gather you from all the nations and from all the places whither I have driven you, saith the Lord, and I will bring you again into the place whence I caused you to be carried away captive. and I will persecute them with the sword, with the famine, and with the pestilence, and will deliver them to be removed to all the kingdoms of the earth, to be a curse, and an astonishment, and an hissing, and a reproach, among all the nations whither I have driven them. Because they have not hearkened to my words, saith the Lord which I sent unto them by my servants the prophets, rising up early and sending them, but ye would not hear, saith the Lord." Jeremiah 29:11-19 KJV*

We hope that your salvation experience is your first experience with your Savior, but we also pray that it is not your last. The word of God is his love letter to you. It is His living, breathing word. We hope you will continue to apply His word to the problem areas of your life and that you have a closer walk with Him. We believe that your personal transformation and the *sanctification* process will take you to heights you never dreamed possible.

We would love to hear your testimony and share your walk with Him. We would love to hear of your stories, and who He is to you: your deliverer, your strength, your high tower, your portion, your husband, your wife, your friend, as you fall more in love with your "Abba Father."

*"Journey of the Soul,"* the *sanctification* process is for those children who have accepted Christ as their Lord and Savior. It is a tool to invite the Lord God to transform your life into the creation you were meant to become. If you do not know the Lord God and have no personal relationship with Christ, you have no power and no indwelling Holy Spirit to assist you on your journey. Accepting Christ as your Savior must be the first step. He is a God of order. Although the gift is free. It became yours when Christ died on the cross and shed his blood for your sins. You must accept it. You must be willing to turn from your sin and self to Christ. You must be willing to make Him the Lord of your life.

If you don't know the Christ that we speak of in *"Journey of the Soul….Cracked Pots and Broken Vessels…"and …."Stop the Violence…Seven Stages to Sanctify,"* if you do not have a personal relationship with Him, if He is not your Abba Father, we invite you to ask Him into your heart today. Right now, this minute, with no fancy words, no preacher, no elaborate prayers, with your own words, tell Him you want to know Him and have a personal relationship with Him. Thank Him for saving you from your sin. Tell Him that you know He is the Son of God come to earth in the flesh to die on the cross for you. Let Him know that you accept the free gift of salvation and eternal life. Let Him know that you want Him to *sanctify* you, heal you and transform you into the vessel He created you to become for His Glory and for your good. Thank Him for forgiving your sins and cleansing you. Let Him know that you turn away from your sin and self to Jesus Christ and ask Him to be the Lord of your life. Amen

Now write down the date on the pages of this book and go back and read *"Journey of the Soul…. Cracked Pots and Broken Vessels…"* and *"Stop the Violence…Seven Stages to Sanctify,"* with the power of God living inside you and watch as the God of the universe turns your darkness into light, your mourning into dancing.

God's first commandment to you after you have accepted Him as your Lord and Savior is to be baptized in the name of the Father, Son and Holy Spirit. You are called to make your decision public before men. *"If you confess me before men, I will confess you before my Father, but if you deny me before men, I will deny you before my Father." Matthew 10:32, 33 Make* a date to be baptized in your local church and become part of the fellowship to help you on your journey. Read the Bible, pray, and spend time with Him in fellowship as He transforms your life into the creation you were meant to become.

## SOME CHARACTERISTICS OF LIVING THE ABUNDANT LIFE CHRIST DIED TO GIVE YOU

Circle the characteristics that you enjoy. Thank God for the gift. Include the transformation in your story... your testimony.

- Accountable to others, not responsible for
- Ordered and balanced
- Joyful
- Creative
- Playful
- Resourceful
- Spontaneous
- Self Actualized (recognizes the gifts and talents from God and uses them)
- On mission
- Intimate relationship with Christ
- Intimacy with others
- Open and honest

✤ Transparent and authentic

✤ Growing in maturity

✤ Glimpses of unconditional love expressed

✤ Congruent: Behavior and words match

✤ Beliefs and values look like Christ

✤ Healthy Boundaries

✤ Safe People

✤ Open system: Information flows in and out

✤ All channels of communication are open

✤ Willingly share thoughts and feelings

✤ Healthy communication skills

✤ Equality in relationships

✤ Knows who they are in Christ

✤ Able to give and receive

✤ Take thoughts captive

✤ Displays of fruits of the Spirit *Galatians 5: 22 KJV "But the fruit of the Spirit is*

✤ *Love, joy, peace, longsuffering, gentleness, goodness, faith, meekness, temperance:"*

**S**trongholds / Sins / Problems          Stage One: Chapter 6

**A**dmit Defenses Used to Cover Pain          Stage Two: Chapter 7

**N**otice Overwhelming Feelings & Thoughts          Stage Three: Chapter 8

**C**ore Issues: Trauma & Abuse          Stage Four: Chapter 9

**T**houghts & Feelings (In Reality)          Stage Five: Chapter 10

**I**dentify Pain / Grieving Process          Stage Six: Chapter 11

**F**reedom : Live the Abundant Life          Stage Seven: Chapter 12

**Y**our Story...Your Testimony...Your Mission          Conclusion: Your Story

# CONCLUSION:

# The Journey is Complete.
# Christ Has Sanctified Another Area of Your Life.

*Christ has come to set the captives free to heal the broken hearted and to bind up the wounds. (Isaiah 6l)*

***Y**our Story…Your Testimony of Freedom in Christ: The Sanctified Area(s) of Your Life.*

***I accept my story and my responsibility to share my testimony with others.***

*The seven stages are completed and the resulting transformation becomes your story, your testimony and your new found freedom in Christ. Each time you have a problem; you can go to the model and allow the Lord to sanctify you in another area of your life. From glory to glory becoming more like Christ, less like the world, as the Lord transforms you into the creature you were meant to become*

**Exercise: Tell Your Story…Your Testimony…Your Mission**

Include each stage of the model and how God transformed and *sanctified* each area of brokenness.

_____

_____

_____

_____

_____

_____

_____

_____

_____

_____

_____

_____

_____

_____

_____

_____

_____

_____

_____

_____

_____

_____

_____

_____

# EPILOGUE:

## Revival Starts with You

*"The Spirit of the Lord is upon me, because he hath anointed me to preach the gospel to the poor; he hath sent me to heal the broken hearted, to preach deliverance to the captives and recovering of sight to the blind, to set at liberty them that are bruised." Luke 4:18 KJV*

*"….Greater works than these shall ye do; because I go unto my Father." John 14:12 b KJV*

If you truly want revival in your churches, communities, states, nation, and country; start with yourself. Individually, you have to make a personal commitment to the Lord Jesus and to your accountability person(s) to strive to be all He created you to be. You must be "doers of the word" and not "hearers only." James 1:22 you must submit to the Lord Jesus in every area of your life. Instead of looking at the "Golden Years" as the place where you are finished; you must see this time as a challenge to go teach, preach and disciple the younger generation.

It is your challenge to model Christ in all you say and do. None of you are capable. There was only one perfect man, Christ. However, you are expected to submit to our Lord and Savior in all aspects of your life as He moves you from glory to glory. You are to study to show yourself approved. (2 Timothy 2:15 KJV) You must set an example for the younger generation by modeling the life He taught you to live. When you are wrong, you must admit your faults, ask for forgiveness and work toward change, with the power of the Holy Spirit. You must examine your life in light of all of God's word and teachings.

Many times you skip over the Old Testament looking to the New Testament because it reflects the state of affairs after Christ's death on the cross and resurrection. However Christ said, *"Think not that I am come to destroy the law, or the prophets: I am not come to destroy, but to fulfill. For verily I say unto you, Till heaven and earth pass, one jot or one title shall in no wise pass from the law, till all be fulfilled."* *Matthew 5:17, 18 KJV*

Christ empowers you through the Holy Spirit to abide by the law, to write it on the tablets of your heart, that you might not sin against Him. If you are His child, you are a son or daughter of the King. He has already given you the gift of power and deliverance; you just have to submit to the *sanctification* process. (Acts 26:18, 1 Corinthians 6:11, 1Thessalonians 4: 3. See also "make holy"). You must first submit yourself to the process of *sanctification* and teach it as an ongoing process that only starts as you walk down the aisle and accept Christ as your Savior.

The promise(s) of the Scriptures, that as you draw near to Him, He will draw near to you, will be fulfilled as you spend time in His word and live in obedience to His teachings. The answers to life's problems are in the instruction book, The Bible, His love letter to you. You must learn how to "rightly apply" the word of God to life's challenges and problems.

Christ's death on the cross, his burial and resurrection have already paid the price for all of your sin(s), diseases, hurts, hang-ups, habits, problems and challenges. The power of the resurrected Jesus flows through your veins as heir to the throne, His child. You must learn to "rightly apply" all of His teachings and claim the abundant life He died to give you.

As Jesus said you must,

*"Go ye therefore, and teach all nations, baptizing them in the name of the Father, and of the Son, and of the Holy Ghost: teaching them to observe all things whatsoever I have commanded you: and, lo, I am with you always, even unto the end of the world. Amen." Matthew 28:19, 20 KJV*

Individual submission to Christ and the *sanctification* process, will lead to stronger marriages, children and families, churches, communities and the nation. The process starts with each one of you being willing to allow Christ, The Holy Spirit in you, to continue the transformation process as you become what He created you to become.

*"I have set before you life and death, blessings and curses; Therefore choose life that both thou and thy seed shall live." Deuteronomy 30:19 KJV*

Discover your story....Learn how to tell it.....Watch God perform miracles in your life as you fall more in love with your "Abba Father."

*"May God himself, the God of peace, sanctify you through and through. May your whole spirit, soul and body be kept blameless at the coming of our Lord Jesus Christ." 1 Thessalonians 5:23*

*We Are "Cracked Pots and Broken Vessels" For His Glory*

# REVEREND CARROL E. DAVIS
# and DR. PHYLLIS E. DAVIS

" *Journey of the Soul…Cracked Pots and Broken Vessels….Living the Victorious Life Christ Died to Give You"* is an expansion of Dr. Phyllis Davis' doctoral studies in Psychology, Applied Theology and a walk with the "Master." Co author, Reverend Carrol Davis takes the basic principles of sound psychological living and combines them with instructions from the "Wonderful Counselor." The resulting seven stage approach helps fellow Christians "rightly divide" the Scriptures in order to overcome problems and challenges of life in a fallen world.

Seven stages take you on a journey to identify the problem, recognize the outward signs, overcome feelings, deal with the real issues, and win over your past, in order to heal your pain and live the victorious life Christ died to give you. Each area of your life that has been *"sanctified"* becomes your story and your testimony of the living Christ and His transformation in your life.

Carrol graduated from Furman University in Greenville, South Carolina in 1975. Carrol was ordained in 1975 as a Baptist minister. He has served as pastor, associate pastor, youth minister, and music minister for over 25 years. He has two grown daughters and a grandson. His hobbies include tinkering with all things mechanical, reading Greek and Latin and an occasional tune on his saxophone.

Phyllis graduated from the University of Texas with a bachelors' degree in business management, radio and television. She received her master's from Antioch University in counseling psychology, marriage and family therapy and her doctorate from the Union Institute in psychology, clinical, organizational, and forensics with special studies in applied theology. Dr. Davis has been honored in Who's Who of American

Women, Who's Who in Science and Engineering, and Who's Who in the World. Since retirement from her private practice and as allied staff for numerous hospitals, she has become involved as a commissioned, licensed prayer minister and biblical counselor. She has two grown children and three grandchildren. She loves the outdoors, the backyard, flowers, and waterfalls.

Together, Rev. Davis and Dr. Davis enjoy teaching and preaching at various organizations including recovery programs, Sunday School(s), workshops, seminars, groups, and in-service trainings for churches and organizations. They believe that they have been called to share their experience, strength and hope and are the authors of *"Journey of the Soul....Cracked Pots and Broken Vessels...Live the Victorious Life Christ Died to Give You"* and the model *"SEVEN STAGES TO SANCTIFY"* on the *sanctification* process. If they are not spending time with family and friends, they love to travel and explore other places, cultures, and culinary delights: mission trips and pleasure cruises. They presently reside in the Carolinas with their "two furry children," Snoopy dog and Tom kitty.

Dr. Phyllis Davis and Rev. Carrol Davis can be contacted for consultation, Bible studies, seminars, and workshops for your church or organization to teach and train on the principles outlined in *"Journey of the Soul....Cracked Pots and Broken Vessels....Live the Victorious Life Christ Died to Give You"©* and the accompanying workbook, *"STOP THE VIOLENCE...SEVEN STAGES TO SANCTIFY...Claim the Promises of Christ"©* containing the model on the *sanctification* process, *"SEVEN STAGES TO SANCTIFY."©* Contact them through Dr. Phyllis E. Davis and Rev. Carrol E. Davis, The Journey Pathways to Healing©, through e-mail: cdavis@thejourneypathwaystohealing.com or carroledavis@gmail.com or pdavis@thejourneypathwaystohealing.com or drphyllisericson@gmail.com or their web site https://www. thejourneypathwaystohealing.net

# "STOP THE VIOLENCE SEVEN STAGES TO SANCTIFY Claim the Promises of Christ"©

## *Seven Stages of the Journey and the Biblical Comparisons©*

*"Work out your salvation with fear and trembling." Philippians 2:12 KJV*

*Salvation and Sanctification: Salvation is a one time event where you invite Christ to be the Lord of your life. Sanctification is a process where you invite the Holy Spirit to mold and shape each area of your life, to transform you from glory to glory, to become more like your Savior. Each area of your life that the Holy Spirit has sanctified becomes one more testimony to God's glory and to your good. Each time you have a problem you can go to the model and allow the Lord to sanctify you in another area of your life: From glory to glory becoming more like Christ, less like the world, as the Lord transforms you into the creature you were meant to become.*

*S Strongholds / Besetting Sins / Problem State*

*I admit that there are areas of my life that do not look like Christ.*

*A Admit Defenses Used To Cover Pain*

*I admit that I use defenses to cover my pain and am not honest and authentic about my feelings.*

*N Notice Overwhelming Feelings/Thoughts*

*I admit that my feelings and thoughts sometimes overwhelm me.*

*C Core Issues: Trauma/Abuse*

*I admit my core issue and face the truth of my history.*

*T Thoughts and Feelings Grounded In Reality:*

*I acknowledge my thoughts and feelings and examine them in light of God's word.*

*I Identify Pain: the Grieving Process*

*I admit my pain and accept healing by grieving my losses.*

*F Freedom to Live the Abundant Life*

*I accept my freedom as a gift from God.*

*Y Your Story…Your Testimony of Freedom in Christ*

# Notes

Ericson, Phyllis, M.A *Co-Dependency, the Disease Concept*. Yellow Springs, Ohio: Antioch University, 1990.

Ericson, Phyllis, M. A. *Journey of the Soul…The Emerging Self*. Ann Arbor, Michigan: U.M.I., Bell & Howell Publishing, 1995.

Davis, Rev. Carrol E. and Davis, Dr. Phyllis E., *Journey of the Soul…Cracked Pots and Broken Vessels… Live the Victorious Life Christ Died to Give You*. Bloomington, Indiana: WestBow Press, a Division of Thomas Nelson and Zondervan Publishing, Inc., 2014.

Davis, Rev. Carrol E. and Davis, Dr. Phyllis E., the model, *"SEVEN STAGES TO SANCTIFY."* Bloomington, Indiana: WestBow Press, a Division of Thomas Nelson and Zondervan Publishing, Inc., 2014.

# Look for Other Works by These Authors

## JOURNEY OF THE SOUL...
## CRACKED POTS AND BROKEN VESSELS...
## Live the Victorious Life Christ Died to Give You.
## DR. PHYLLIS DAVIS and REV. CARROL DAVIS

*"Journey of the Soul...Cracked Pots and Broken Vessels...Live the Victorious Life Christ Died to Give You."...is the companion book to this workbook. Over fifty years of research in the fields of psychology, theology, and recovery combine these sound principles and the words of the Master to offer an alternative to "talk therapy." This unique approach combines right brain techniques to go to the root of problems addressing the cause rather than treating symptoms only. The book is a discipleship tool to help Christians mature in Christ while overcoming problems and challenges of life in a fallen world.*

*The JOURNEY© techniques have received world wide acclaim in acknowledging Dr. Phyllis Davis in Who's Who in the World, Who's Who in Science and Engineering, and Who's Who in American Women. Available on line and through the publisher, WestBow Press, a division of Thomas Nelson and Zondervan Publishing: (866) 928-1240, www.WestBow Press.com the online bookstore*

*"JOURNEY of the Soul…Cracked Pots and Broken Vessels…Live the Victorious Life Christ Died to Give You." Dr. Phyllis Davis and Rev. Carrol Davis*

# Appendix A:

# *RELEASE FORMS MUST BE FILLED OUT BY ALL ATTENDEES TO THE WORKSHOP

**I _____agree to the confidentiality of all persons attending the workshop and agree not to disclose who is in attendance, nor the nature of the discussions. All information is confidential. What is said here stays here. If I choose to break this agreement, I understand that the choice is grounds for dismissal without refund of my donation.

The following information is for the treatment team to better assist me with the issues I am working on. I know that the information is confidential for this purpose. I release this information to be used accordingly.

I understand that Dr. Phyllis E. Davis is an educated psychologist, commissioned prayer minister and that Rev. Carrol E. Davis is an ordained minister. They operate under the licenses of Christian Counselor(s) and Ordained Minister(s). The counseling is Christian counseling based on the word of God.

I_____ hereby release Dr. Phyllis E. Davis and Rev. Carrol E. Davis to contact my other doctor(s) as is necessary for consultation, treatment and in case of emergency.

Signed this the _____day of _____, 2014.

_____          _____

Signature of Attendee (date) _____          Signature of Witness (date) _____

Disclosures and acknowledgement:

\*\*All information is confidential and is to be reviewed by the treatment team only for purposes of biblical, Christian counseling. EXCEPTION TO THE CONFIDENTIALITY RULE IS IF YOUR LIFE OR THE LIFE OF ANOTHER IS THREATENED, or IN DANGER, VIOLATION OF THE LAWS OF THE STATE, OR FEDERAL GOVERNMENT, AND THE REQUIREMENT TO REPORT E. g. Abuse of children and /or the elderly require reporting and suspected harm of self and/or others.

\*We are a 501c3 organization. Donations received may be tax deductible. Talk with your CPA or accountant. Benefits received are for intangible religious benefits.

# Appendix B

*INTAKE SHEET FOR THE JOURNEY PATHWAYS TO HEALING, REV. CARROL DAVIS AND DR. PHYLLIS DAVIS (864) 449-4867. CONTACT US BY E-MAIL carroledavis@gmail.com or drphyllisericson@gmail.com or see our web sites: thejourneypathwaystohealing.com or thejourneypathwaystohealing.net.

## PERSONAL INFORMATION

Name_____ (Last, First, Middle)

Address_____ (Home)(Include Zip)

E-Mail Address_____

Telephone_____ (Home)_____(Cell)

Employer_____

Business Address_____

Business Position_____

Referred By_____

Age ____Sex _____Height _____Weight_____

Date of Birth _____Place of Birth_____

Religion _____Church Member

Yes_____No____Where?_____

Church Address_____

Have You Been Saved ? _____When?_____

Have You Been Baptized? _____ When? _____

Please comment about your religious experience:

_____

_____

_____

_____

_____

_____

_____

Education: Years Completed_____ Degrees/Courses earned_____

Occupation _____How long at present job?_____

*Do you feel comfortable about your occupational efforts? _____Yes _____No

Explain:

_____

_____

_____

_____

_____

_____

Military Service: Dates_____ Primary Task_____

Do you suffer from PTSD? _____ Yes _____No If Yes, explain below briefly:

Explain _____

Physician_____Address_____

_____ Phone_____

Psychiatrists or Psychologist_____Address_____

_____Phone_____

How long since you have had a check-up_____

Any physical or mental limitations we should know about? _____

Previous counseling and/or Psychiatric care _____When? _____

Doctor, Counselor, Hospital _____ Address_____

Are you currently being treated for a condition? _____ If so, explain below: _____

_____

_____

_____

_____

_____

_____

List any medications you are currently taking and the condition for which they are prescribed:

| Medication | How many milligrams? | What is the medication for? |
|---|---|---|
| | How often taken? | |

_____

_____

_____

_____

_____

_____

## *FAMILY SITUATION

Present status: Single_____      Engaged since _____Separated since_____

Divorced since_____      Married      since      _____Widowed

since_____

Previous marriages: Number _____Broken by: Divorce (date) _____ Death (date) _____

Other:_____

_____

Mate: First name _____ Mate: Last name _____

Date of Birth _____Education _____Occupation_____

Religion_____ Hobbies _____

Spouse's Employer _____

Type of business _____ Position _____

Descriptive comments: _____

_____

Are you or have you been a victim of spouse abuse? Yes_____ When? _____ No _____

Children: Note if any of the children are from a blended family and/or a previous marriage

| First Name | Boy/Girl | Age | School Grade | Descriptive | Comment |
|---|---|---|---|---|---|
| | | | | | |
| | | | | | |
| | | | | | |
| | | | | | |
| | | | | | |
| | | | | | |
| | | | | | |

*Who is currently living in your household? _____

Are your parents living together? Yes_____ No _____ Separated _____ Divorced? _____

Deceased? Mother _____Father? _____ Stepmother? _____

Stepfather? _____ Sibling? _____ Close Friend? _____

| Parents: | Mother | Father |
|---|---|---|
| Education | | |
| Occupation | | |

Religious Preference _____

Descriptive Comments: _____

Approved of your marriage _____

Before _____

Later _____

Rate your parents' marriage: Very happy _____ Happy _____ So-So _____ Unhappy _____

Do you feel closest to your: Father _____ Mother _____ Others _____

I was born number _____ of _____ children.

List order of birth (oldest to youngest) of your sisters or brothers and include yourself.

| First Name | Boy or Girl | Age | Descriptive Comments |
|---|---|---|---|
| _____ | _____ | ____ | _____ |
| _____ | _____ | ____ | _____ |
| _____ | _____ | ____ | _____ |
| _____ | _____ | ____ | _____ |
| _____ | _____ | ____ | _____ |
| _____ | _____ | ____ | _____ |
| _____ | _____ | ____ | _____ |

From what source did you receive sex information? _____

*Were you abused as a child? Yes __ No __ Physically? __ Sexually? ___ Emotionally? __ Intellectually? ___

Give any other information about your family that was significant for you, stressful or traumatic such as:

Life adjustments, health, education, vacations, accidents, economic situation, moving, etc:

_____

_____

_____

_____

_____

_____

Has life been satisfying to you? _____ Explain _____

_____

_____

_____

List present physical complaints

_____

_____

Has there been any important change in your body in the past year? _____ Describe: _____

_____

Has your weight changed as much as ten pounds in the past year? _____

List previous illnesses and /or problems that caused special stress? _____

_____

_____

_____

_____

_____

_____

Have you lost someone or something of major importance to you in the last five years? Describe:

_____

_____

_____

Have you ever attempted suicide? _____ When? _____ Method? _____

*Why have you chosen this time to use counseling to work on your situation? _____

_____

_____

_____

List present problems in order of importance

_____

_____

_____

Additional comments

_____

_____

_____

_____

_____

_____

Body Symptoms and Somatic Pain: Do you now have any of the following symptoms? Circle all that apply. Circle and check all that apply and are regular problems.

Tension headaches

Migraine headaches

Other headaches

Allergies

Sinus infection

Post nasal drip

Thyroid trouble

High blood pressure

Low blood pressure

Pain in chest

Tightness in chest

Heaviness on chest

Heart trouble

*Difficulty with breathing

Knots or cramps in the stomach

Ulcer

Stiff neck

Stiffness in shoulders

Backache

Constipation

Diarrhea

Kidney trouble

Colon trouble

Hemorrhoids

Impotence

Frigidity

Vasectomy

Miscarriage

Menstrual trouble

Hysterectomy

Vaginitis

Yeast infections

Syphilis

Pain in legs or feet

Fainting spells

Convulsions

Paralysis

Shaking

Bone trouble

Nerve trouble

*Insomnia

Fatigue

Appetite loss

Tumors

Cancer

Diabetes

Asthma

Alcoholism

Drug Addiction

Do you have any symptoms not covered above? _____ If yes, describe below:

_____

_____

_____

Are you now or have you ever been a member of a secretive organization? Yes_____ No_____

If yes, describe the organization _____Are you still active? Yes _____No _____

Did any of your family members belong to a secretive organization? Yes _____ No _____

If yes, describe the organization _____ Are they still active? Yes_____ No____

## *WRITTEN DISCLOSURE AND ACKNOWLEDGEMENT

We are licensed Christian counselors providing guidance based on the word of God, the Bible.
We are a 501 C 3 organization. Donations received can be tax deductible. Talk with your accountant or CPA as services are for intangible religious benefit.

# "STOP THE VIOLENCE...SEVEN STAGES TO SANCTIFY...Claim the Promises of Christ©"

## *World wide recognition...treats the root cause...not just the symptoms*

Testimonies

"Very well-conceived; goes beyond academic exercises and focuses on self-awareness and deep reflection; honesty and faith." Editor of a Leading Christian Publishing Co.

"I just know your new books will help a lot of people." Leader Christ-Based Recovery Program. Industry Owner/Leader

"You are very good at expressing yourself and your ideas." Retired Instructor Journalism Department: Major Christian University

"I have never before experienced this kind of resolution in counseling. Thank you." Former Patient, Previously Misdiagnosed for Over 5 years

Rev. Carrol Davis and Dr. Phyllis Davis

"Authors/ Speakers/ Consultants/ Trainers"

The JOURNEY Pathways to Healing©

(864) 449-4867 or email carroledavis@gmail.com

*Seminars *Staff Trainings *Marriage Retreats* Groups

©copyright 1993, 1995, revised 2013, 2014

Printed in the USA
CPSIA information can be obtained
at www.ICGtesting.com
LVHW080748190823
755700LV00045B/1454

9 781629 5275